Now What?

For Families with Trans
and Gender-Nonconforming Children

Rex Butt, Ph.D.

Cover design by Scott Smith.

First published by Dog Ear Publishing
4010 W. 86th Street, Ste H
Indianapolis, IN 46268
www.dogearpublishing.net

ISBN: 978-1-4575-1625-2

This book is printed on acid-free paper.

Printed in the United States of America

TABLE OF CONTENTS

FOREWORD

For the past two decades I have been privileged to work as a therapist and advocate with many trans people, of all ages and from many backgrounds. They have been formidable teachers for me about how to live with dignity and respect in a social world that constantly "others" and "disappears" trans people, and mostly simply misunderstands them. At first, I worked primarily with older transsexual woman and crossing dressing men who were coming out later in life, and often actualizing themselves at the cost of losing long-term marriages and rejection from children. Later, I began to mostly see younger transmen seeking treatment, often shedding lesbian identities, and leaving communities that had been sources of strength to find greater comfort in their bodies. In the past few years, the phone has literally been ringing off the hook, from parents of young children who are expressing gender-nonconforming behavior. Parents struggling with whether to let their son grow his hair and play with Barbies; parents struggling with how to support a child (including grown children) wanting to start taking cross-sex hormones. It is clear that transgender and gender non-conforming people exist across the spectrum of humanity, and are challenging parents, families, schools, and communities to expand our consciousness about sex and gender.

In my practice, Choices Counseling and Consulting located in Albany, New York, we provide a support group for parents. We (my staff and I) provide services for over 40 families who have children who are gender-variant or transgender identified. The children range from 5 to 40 years old. At first I thought, "What would a parent of a small child who is gender-variant have in common with a parent of transsexual adult?" The answer is a resounding, "A LOT!" I rarely plan "group exercises" or "ice breakers" so common in therapeutic groups. The families don't seem to need help talking with one another. Across race, and age, and religion and class, and so many other cultural variables, the room is inevitable full of laughter and tears, as well as anger and fears.

For too long parents have been isolated addressing the needs of gender non-conforming children. In the book, *What to Expect When you are Expecting*, there is no section on gender, not a word on children born with intersex conditions, nor a discussion alluding to the fact that the sex assigned at birth is not always correct. Parents dutifully paint children's bedrooms pink and blue, and follow the arrows to the "boys" and "girls" sections of *Toys R US*, and spend most of their time worrying about food allergies, bicycle helmets, and child molesters. We have spent far too little time thinking about our children's gender: gender roles, gender expression, gender identity, gender acquisition, and gender oppression. Or what Diane Ehrensaft, author of *Gender Born, Gender Made*, refers to as "gender *health*."

I recently made a trip to my son's elementary school. He is a "big kid" (a sixth grader), but as I entered the school, I saw first grader's walking down the hall – a line of children, boys on one side, girls on the other. The girls were a sparkling array of pinks and purples, shimmery, glittery shirts, blouses, skirts, pants, all patterns and sequins, with dangling accouterments – bracelets, headbands, pocketbooks – skipping, sauntering, and dancing down the hall. The boys all wore browns, blues and blacks. They all wore t-shirts, blue jeans, and sneakers. They plodded along in the line, nary a song in their step. There, I thought, is our culture with gender rules in action. I looked to see if there was one girl rejecting the hot pink glitter, or one boy with more flair, but they scuttled off too quickly.

Years ago, when my children were younger, we attended an end-of-summer camp play. The boys and girls performed different skits. The girls were dressed in skimpy clothes, doing a flirtatious dance, wiggling their fannies at the audience. The boys did a military march, complete with fake guns. We were the only parents to complain apparently, the only ones who thought these gendered polarities were inappropriate messages to send to 4 and 5 year old children.

Most people simply do not think much about gender. Not unless our children insist that we do. And an increasing number of parents are having children that do insist, even demand, that gender become a central focus of the lives of our families.

Let's be honest: as oppressive and arbitrary as most gender rules are, most children, more or less, play by the rules. Perhaps a boy is not particularly sports inclined, or a girl eschews all the glitter, but by and large, most people find a comfort zone within the existing societal rules and do not question them (much). For some families they are therefore shocked when an adult child emails a long letter saying that they are transsexual. Parents are often saying, "This is completely out of the blue. He was a perfectly *normal* little boy." Normal, typical, usual, average ... perhaps on the outside, but on the inside "he" carried a secret – and never really fit in.

Some children express gender atypical behaviors from the time they are small. This is most evident if the parent has other children who did not veer from the established path. For many liberal parents, reared themselves on feminism, they took this in stride, and provided more gender neutral toys and games. For some parents, more conservative and traditional, and perhaps more religious, the expectations for gender are more clearly demarcated, and the child's transgressions do not appear cute, but defiant and inappropriate. In some families, the gender atypicality goes underground, either because the family insists on it, or because the child chooses to go along with social expectations and peer pressure. The behaviors witnessed at three and five have disappeared at seven. Parents say that the child has "outgrown" them, and professionals call them "desisters," those whose gender nonconformity has stopped. No one knows at this stage, whether these experiences will re-emerge in puberty of adulthood.

Other children become increasingly gender nonconforming as they mature. The little boy who liked pink ponies and preferred art to soccer becomes nearly obsessed with dressing up as a girl and decorating his room in vibrant colors. He keeps asking grandma to call him a girl. The little girl who always liked her hair short and never wore dresses enters puberty and begins hiding and even binding her breasts and choosing a male "nickname." Far more worrisome is the depression, the rage fits, the anxiety and OCD behaviors, the suicidal gestures, and self-harm behaviors. Parents worry about drugs, alcohol, and eating disorders, and watching their children suffer is perhaps the greatest pain the world.

A decade ago I could not have imagined how often parents could say, hopefully, "Maybe my child is gay." Indeed it seems that "gay liberation" has come so far that being gay is now a positive outcome, a resolution that can inspire and provide hope. And surely it is possible that gender-variant children will grow up to identify as gay, lesbian, or bisexual—indeed the research confirms that this is a likely outcome. What is unknown, and what no professional can prophecy, is which children will desist, which will persist, which will identify as gay, and which will want to affirm a cross-gender identity.

So parents are left, as we always have been, since we dreamed our children into existence—we have to love them as they are, and allow them to become who they will. A tall order while we try to get them to do their homework, not pick their nose in public, and put their dirty socks in the laundry. In so many areas of life our job is to direct and teach but when we "do gender" with our kids we must reflect, learn, and provide endless love.

My friend and colleague Jean Malpas says, "Families of gender nonconforming children need to negotiate the interactions between two gender systems: a rigid gender binary imported from familial, social and cultural experiences and a fluid gender spectrum articulated by their child." There have been few books to help parents do. Rex Butt has written such a book, one to help parents negotiate the complexities of having a child who does not easily fit into society's gender boxes.

This book: *Now What? For Families with Trans and Gender-Nonconforming Children*, is easy to read, offering solace, comfort, advice, and experience to assist parents in negotiating this minefield of parenting gender non-conforming children. This book provides critical background information for families and practical suggestions, including how to manage coming out to family and friends; how to manage ongoing stress, especially as children near puberty; and how to keep communication open during stressful times with children of all ages. This is a much needed book and one I can finally hand to parents who ask, *"Now What?"*

Arlene Istar Lev LCSW-R, CASAC
Albany, New York
www.choicesconsulting.com

ACKNOWLEDGMENTS

There is always a danger in offering acknowledgements because no book is ever completed through the efforts of one person, and it is difficult for me to recall all the people who have helped to make this book possible.

The parents and therapists who agreed to be interviewed for this book helped to establish what needed to be covered, and without their openness and insight, I would have been left to merely guess from my family's experience what others need to know.

I thank the City University of New York for approving the sabbatical that allowed me time for those interviews and the bulk of the research. That research was supported primarily by two libraries and their staff members who accommodated an endless stream of queries and requests. I especially appreciate the support that I received from the inter-library loan team at the Poughkeepsie Public Library and the tireless and gracious digging of Thomas Riker, the Collection Management Librarian for Bronx Community College.

Ari Lev was extremely helpful and generous with her time and expertise, as was my diligent and drastically underpaid editor, Elizabeth Segal.

On a personal level, I thank the transgender people who have been so open and welcoming to my questions. I thank them for letting me be part of their lives. I thank Donna Festa, who rescued my kid and helped her to find who she is. I also thank my family and Karen's family for their support and understanding.

This book would never have gotten written without my wife Karen's encouragement and occasional badgering. Finally, I thank my children, Cadence, whose courage, patience and wit has led our family into the unknown and Chad, who has been a rock of love and support for his sister and his parents—indeed for everyone in his life.

PREFACE

This book has been written primarily for parents of transgender and gender-nonconforming children, regardless of age. Whether your child is three or fifty-three, this book is for you. Of course, others may find this book helpful as well. The strategies and the research discussed here are likely to be helpful to siblings and other family members—even for transgender people themselves.

Since you're reading this book, there's a good chance that you want to find some answers. Although I can't guarantee that you'll find answers to all your questions here, you're likely to find your questions explored, and you'll see how others have answered their questions. This book is designed to provide information so that you can discover your own answers. There is no preaching here—well, there is some, but I've worked to issue a warning when it happens.

When our child came out to us as transsexual in 2002, Karen and I didn't really know what it meant. We knew what a transsexual was, but we didn't know what it meant for our family. We were full of questions: How could this happen? Does it mean surgery? How can she be so sure? What caused this? Is it our fault? How can we handle all this? Is it real? How can we keep our child safe? Where will this end? How will we tell others and who should we tell?

Of course, the list was longer than that. In fact, it is still growing.

You may not find that particularly comforting. After all, you are reading this book to get answers, not to hear that the questions never stop, but it's important that you know up front what this book provides, and, just as important, what it does not provide.

First, I have no credentials that mark me as an expert in issues of gender. I'm not a licensed psychologist or a social worker. I don't even have a degree in gender studies or psychology. As a result, you won't find me telling you what to do.

So what do I have to offer you? I have interviewed or mentored well over one hundred parents of transsexual or gender-nonconforming children. All names in reference to those parents and their families have been changed throughout. I have read well over four hundred books and articles in preparation for this book. I also have spent nearly two decades researching and teaching interpersonal communication. Given that background, I can say with authority that I am aware of the most common problems that families face when confronted with this issue and how people can work through those problems productively. The first three chapters of the book focus on those problems. I also offer you assurance that I have distilled the research that has been conducted on transgender issues and on interpersonal effectiveness. In the last three chapters, I present that research so that it makes sense.

Chapter one explains the ways in which parents have discovered that their child is transgender through situations recounted in interviews with parents. It identifies behaviors that have indicated gender nonconformity and how parents have responded to those behaviors. It helps to put your emotional responses into perspective by showing the variety of responses that others have had, and it offers first-step options to help you avoid unwarranted assumptions, and it outlines strategies to help you cope effectively.

Chapter two helps you to determine how to reach out to others, to sort out who needs to know, how much they need to know, and when they need to know. It provides examples of mistakes that others have made and lays out guidelines to help you to avoid common pitfalls. It provides strategies to avoid setting yourself up for rejection and offers a model about how to "come out" to family and friends in ways that encourage supportive responses. It also works through the tension between the need for privacy and the desire to be "out" so that you can live your life authentically. Finally, it helps you to find ways to balance your needs and those of your child.

Chapter three provides definitions of terms and an explanation of how transsexualism has been treated in the United States. It explains the diagnosis of Gender Identity Disorder (GID) from the *Diagnostic and Statistical Manual of Mental Disorders* (DSM) and how that diagnosis is used in therapy and medical treatment. It explains possible medical interventions, including hormone blockers, hormone therapy, and the variety of surgical options to consider.

Chapter four helps you to explore and assuage feelings of guilt. Starting with examples of the guilt other parents have felt and how they came to terms with it, the chapter explains how the history of psychological theory in the U.S. has exacerbated the problem by assessing blame on parents, almost always mothers, and their choices in child rearing. It explains theories about the possible causes of gender nonconformity then concludes with a summary of theories that challenge the validity of the nature/nurture debate, furnishing evidence that nature and nurture are not as separate as we assume.

Chapter five taps into my years of teaching and researching effective communication and shows you ways to maintain open communication with your gender-nonconforming child and with your family and friends. It outlines how the process has unfolded for others and highlights the potential sources of mental and emotional distress for you and your family. The chapter provides strategies to help you to deal with other people's reactions. It shows ways to produce ongoing positive interactions with others, regardless of their initial or extended responses. Finally, it explains how to confront hostile or uninformed reactions openly without becoming defensive or putting others on the defensive.

Chapter six offers perspectives and traditions from other cultures and dispels myths that the U.S. culture is the worst possible culture for gender-nonconforming people. It explains cultural attitudes and assumptions about gender nonconformity in a variety of cultures, including Thailand, India, the Balkans, Western Europe, and Native American cultures. It finishes with an examination of the current controversy regarding revision of the DSM.

My goal is to provide you with all the basic knowledge you need to come to grips with what your family is facing and how you can work through the challenges that come your way. This book should help you no matter how much you currently know or don't know. If some of the terms in this introduction are foreign to you, relax. You will find them explained as your read.

If you don't find answers to all of your questions, or if you want to dig deeper, I'll be referring you to sources so that you can read further if you want to. Rather than expecting you to accept my conclusions, I provide access to the sources that I have read so that you can investigate further if you wish to.

One final note: there is no right way to read this book. I'd love to have your read it through, but if a chapter description above calls to you, that's the place to go. I've tried to avoid jargon that would get in your way, but at times it serves as an efficient shorthand. If you get confused, please note that chapter three offers an extensive alphabetical glossary of terms.

My hope is that you will find it useful and that it will help your family move forward productively, and lovingly. For us it's been a journey that has created anxieties and frustrations but also profound growth and a deep appreciation for the endless stream of possibilities that life offers us if we allow ourselves to recognize them and embrace them.

CHAPTER 1

Climbing outside the Box

"It's a girl!"

THOSE WORDS BEGIN OUR FORMULATION of perceptions and assumptions about our child in profound, often unrecognized and unacknowledged ways. Even parents who raise their children with a conscious effort to eliminate gender stereotypes inadvertently reinforce deeply entrenched cultural norms. Without realizing it, mothers interact with female children and male children in very different ways, encouraging "gross motor activities . . . and higher rates of activity and physical prowess" in boys.[1] Consciously or unconsciously, we steer girls toward cooperative patterns of behavior and boys toward hierarchical ones.[2]

When such dichotomous habits are so heavily ingrained in our interactions, we seldom if ever recognize them in ourselves. It is tempting and, unfortunately, quite common to simplify our thinking by creating false dualities: on/off, up/down, boy/girl, pink/blue, man/woman, feminine/masculine, heterosexual/homosexual. This sort of thinking may provide comfort in that when we label something we put it in a mental box so that we know where to find it. If we stuff a person in a box, we know who they fit in with, and we know where to look for them the next time we think of them. What we gain through such simplistic thinking is certainty rather than accuracy or clarity, and when we limit our perceptions through the restrictive lens of certainty, we eliminate variation, complexity and nature. We tend to use a short list of traits to describe our children—this one is the smart one, that one the witty one, that one the prankster. None of this is necessarily true. It's all in our heads. But we are very adept at finding evidence for the traits we assign to others, and the more evidence we amass in support of these simplistic assumptions, the more confident we become that the boxes we put people in are somehow based in reality rather than in our imagination.

Challenges to our boxes can be relatively easy to accept with insignificant matters or people: "Okay, so only in bookish ways is she the smart one," or "It doesn't matter whether he's that cynical. I don't really spend any time around him or care about him." But we have a harder time when deeply buried assumptions are challenged by those dear to us: "What can she possibly mean, she's a boy? I changed her diaper. I know what she is."

We want nothing more than to keep people in the boxes that we have created for them, yet we often battle the limitations of the boxes others have put us in. We all struggle with this, some more mightily than others. From our earliest awareness of self, we recognize the comforts and constraints of these boxes. There is a great sense of belonging and ease when we know that we fit in with others. I, for example, am quite comfortable with parts of my PFLAG-dad box.[3] It provides me with a sense of collegiality with my fellow members, and it demonstrates my support for my child. But the box can be limiting. If nothing else, it distances me from people who might assume that I am a militant advocate and that I look down upon them in their struggles to accept and support their child's status as gay or gender-nonconforming.

Imagine, though, that you have been stuck in a box that offers no comfort, that it is lined with unforgiving thorns on all sides. What is worse, you have spent so much time among these thorns that they are familiar to you, perversely comfortable in their familiarity. You may want to climb out, but you've been thrown back in so many times that you've almost given up and are beginning to accept that perhaps everyone else is right and that you actually belong here after all. If even your parents insist that you don't know who you are, you begin to doubt your ability to sort out what is real.

I have not experienced such comprehensive rejection of my sense of self, so I can only guess, but the level of frustration and self-doubt that it provokes might be akin to what gender-nonconforming people face. Regardless of age, the experience must be excruciating. If I were to come up against it at the age of three, the world would seem a very threatening, hostile place. I would feel powerless. If I were finally to realize at the age of forty that the decades of suffering were caused not by my own freakishness but by the prickly box that others had forced me into, I think I'd be pretty angry. I would have an intense urge to strike out at anyone who took part in stuffing me into that box, particularly my parents.

But parents themselves are in a box. We are continuously judged by others in their response to the behavior of our children, and when a child does something so outrageous that it embarrasses us and offends others, we want to tamp down the behavior. It seems that the least that we should expect is that our child would stay in the boy box or the girl box, but more and more, we find children are climbing out of even those boxes, and they are doing it at all ages.

In this chapter, we will look at how several parents have learned about their child's gender nonconformity and how they have responded. First, we have Jessica, a resident of the United Kingdom, who sensed very early on that her child needed support.

> From eighteen months—maybe around two years—he always gravitated toward girl things. He was my first child, and I expected him to show the sort of behavior that I had seen in my nephews and my friends' children, and he just didn't. She seemed more sensitive, and wanted to play with soft toys. By the time she was two and a half, she wanted Barbies and dolls and was not interested in trucks like her older cousins. I questioned it a little bit, but she would put sweaters on her head to pretend she had long hair. I thought it was just a phase.
>
> The pre-school staff alerted me that my child was playing dress up with aprons while the other little boys were going to the capes and the fireman outfits. I said that I was aware of it and to let her get on with it. I spoke to her doctor when she was four because she said, "God made a mistake. I should be a girl," and when she said it to me, it seemed very profound, maybe because I already knew something was going on. The doctor said some children can exhibit gender-variant behavior, that it could be a phase and I should not worry but should keep an eye on her. About then, I had a second child, and the differences in basic behavior were obvious. By the time Jordon was eighteen months old, he was very much a boy,

always wanting to kick a ball around and loving rough-and-tumble play.

Meanwhile, Curtis was hating being in his own skin. I spoke to the doctor again, and he referred me to the local mental health service.[4] They said there was nothing to do unless parents could agree. Well, my husband wanted to stop the behavior, so for a few months I tried to do the Canadian thing where you steer them back to male behavior. But it was just destroying her. She became very quiet and depressed and you could see that she felt that she was a bad person, that there was something wrong with her. She'd had feedback from other kids: "Why do you like those things? You're a boy." So, she already felt bad about herself, and now the two people who were supposed to be always there for her were doing the very same thing.

She became very quiet, very introverted.

I realized that this was the wrong thing to do. We were making this child feel that she was a bad person for something that she couldn't change. She wasn't seeking attention or acting out. She was just miserable and very down, but still insisting that she had a girl brain in a boy body. So I gave it up and said, "It's okay to feel this way. You might feel differently when you are bigger." I was sick of trying to make her "perform" so that other people felt better. It got better, but at six, she asked for the operation to cut off her willy and get a fanny. She ran away from school to get home because she wanted to be where she felt safe. Unless you've actually lived with it, I don't think anyone knows how it feels to be with someone who, day in and day out, can't stand the body that they are in. It is painful to watch.

Obviously, Jessica was attuned to Curtis's discomfort, and it probably helped that she had Jordan's behavior for comparison, which enabled her to see how restrictive male gender expectations were for Curtis. Yet, despite her sensitivity to his needs she failed to understand the mammoth proportion of thorns in the "boy" box she and others had been foisting on him. As she points out, Curtis was being forced to "perform" a role for the sake of others that was so painful he had to escape, so he just shut down. Jessica's explanation of the Canadian model refers to the work of Kenneth Zucker and a team of psychologists in Toronto's Centre for Addiction and Mental Health. Zucker has been accused of coercing gender-nonconforming children to conform to societal norms and is scorned by most of the transgender community. A more complete exploration of Zucker's methods is offered in chapter two, but for now let us accept Jessica's choice of the word *steer* as reasonably accurate.

The father's attitude is an important factor. Jessica reports that his original response along with that of his family was that she was "making it worse" and that Curtis should "get on with being a boy." Fortunately, when Curtis's discomfort became more dire, her husband agreed with her assessment that Curtis was spiraling downward and needed to have his behavior confirmed rather than redirected. They both supported Curtis, who transitioned at age nine, wearing feminine clothing, playing with the toys that brought pleasure and assuming the name of Kristen. Therapists, regardless of their approach to the treatment of gender nonconformity in children, recognize the need for a united front on the part of parents. The situation is already confusing and upsetting for the child, and mixed messages from Mom and Dad only heighten the child's anxiety.

But denial and disbelief are not solely the province of fathers. It is not unusual for any parent to insist upon what appears to be obvious even if that insistence denies the child's perception. If we are resourceful, however, we can open doors for children even after we have unwittingly slammed them closed previously. Witness Monette's example:

> Before the age of two, I remember thinking she never was a typical boy and that I'm probably going to have a gay son. But I thought, "That's ridiculous! He's not even two. Stop thinking that way."
>
> He never liked boy toys—always went to his older sister's room to play with Barbie. I had friends who would say when you have a boy it's so different, but I was saying, "This is not different at all."
>
> By the time he could walk—well, maybe about 16 months, he'd go into the kitchen, open the drawer and put a towel on his head. My mom would come and visit and ask, "What is he doing?" and I would say, "I don't know. He just likes to run around with a towel on his head."

I remember taking him swimming, and he did not want to take his shirt off. I would tell him, "It's okay, honey. Boys can take their shirts off," but we would have to force him to do it.

At about two and a half he started saying, "I'm a girl! I'm not a boy!" and he was very serious.

I said, "No, Sweetie, you're a boy." And this kept bothering me, so I went on the computer for "when your boy says he's a girl" and gender identity disorder came up, I was surprised that there was even a term for it, but I never put in "transgender" because I thought that referred to gay people. So I got my husband and I said, "Don, look at this." We were glad to know that there were other parents going through the same thing, but we were still wishing that it was a phase that would go away.

In my family we would joke that Teddy is already gay, but a friend who is a school psychologist said, "It's not a matter of being gay; it's GID."

I said, "I know, I've already looked it up," but it didn't really sink in. When he was in kindergarten, I asked him, "Are you feeling better about being a boy?"

He said, "No, Mommy, I'm not."

So I said, "Look, don't worry about being a boy or a girl. Just be Teddy."

Although not mean-spirited, Monette's original reaction was a direct denial of Teddy's assertion that he was a girl. After having the time to gain perspective, Monette found a means of relating to him in a way that might help alleviate some of the stress that he is feeling. During our interview, it was clear that Monette was quite intelligent and also very supportive of her child, but she clearly had struggled with accepting what she had read and what her friend reinforced, possibly because the description of gender identity disorder that she read may not have matched all the behavior that she had seen in Teddy.

Reading about gender nonconformity does not necessarily prepare us to recognize it in our own child, and personal exposure to transsexualism is no guarantee of acceptance either. Witness our next mom, Reagan, who had encountered transsexuals in her work as a life coach, and also expressed denial when, after years of emotional turmoil, her fourteen-year-old daughter finally told her what was happening.

My initial reaction was . . . I don't even know if I can describe it. Shock! Shock to the point of an out-of-body sort of feeling. Not because I had any strong feelings about transsexualism or any sort of difference because I don't. But shock. I couldn't take it in at that point. But we talked and she cried and I cried. But I didn't sleep. The thoughts that were going through my head were, "Can this be? People get confused all the time in adolescence about sexuality." That was before I understood about sexuality as being distinct from gender. . . . The next few days were just sort of quiet. I remember saying to her, "We should take our time. People do get confused in puberty," and she was really very patient with me.

Reagan had worked with transsexuals and was accepting of them, yet her first assumption was that her child was speaking from a confused teenager's perspective. Contrary to what Reagan assumed, teenagers who identify as transsexuals generally have a very clear idea about their status, but being well aware of how taboo the topic is, they are likely to hold back. It is understandable that when they finally cannot endure hiding any longer, they might struggle to express what they are feeling. That does not, however, necessarily mean that the feeling itself is vague or ill-defined.

A parent's use of pronouns can be a powerful part of this denial. The three cases that we have explored so far may have created a bit of confusion—who are we talking about, a *he* or a *she*? I interviewed each of these mothers well after she had come to accept her child as having transitioned to the other gender. Jessica moved from male to female pronouns as she explored the moments in the past in which she had learned of Kristen's gender nonconformity, but, aside from when she was recounting early childhood incidents, each mother consistently used *she* and *her* in reference to her child even though the child had been originally raised as a boy. It is difficult, however, to assure that you have actually "turned the corner" on pronouns. My trans daughter,[5] Cadence, came out to us over eight years ago, and Karen and I are proudly consistent in our use of female pronouns—until our younger son Chad, who is three years younger, arrives for a visit. From the moment he enters the house we begin to stumble again with many a *h . . . she* and *hi . . . her*. Although we don't revert back to her old name, residual male pronouns rattle around the house for few days after Chad's departure. Luckily for us, Cadence is forgiving and sometimes even claims not to have noticed discrepancies.

Like Reagan, Karen and I are fortunate to have a child who has indulged us as we scale the learning curve. But patience with the parents while they catch on may not be the norm. As another mom explains, "It's like running laps. By the time we found out what was up, Landon had been around the track plenty of times, but he wants us to catch up immediately even though he's still running—and he's younger than we are."

Come along for a run on this track. You jog on to join your daughter—at least you have always thought of her as your daughter—who is finishing her tenth lap. You are running beside her, and it certainly seems that you are together, experiencing the same moment, but your child is actually several miles ahead of you on this run and she knows the track well. She knows to avoid the mushy inside lane at the north turn. She knows when apparent fatigue will give way to her second wind, which is now allowing her to coast along as you labor beside her. She also has graduated from wearing a sports bra to binding her breasts, and she is very likely to have been researching details on the Internet for several months prior to inviting you to join her.

When your child is ten laps ahead of you on this track, your naive sense of disorientation can read like brazen denial to her. You may think that you are innocently wondering, "Are you sure?" but she hears, "You're only fifteen, and you don't know what you are talking about." In this situation, you may simply want to catch up, but your anxiety and lack of knowledge shows through to your child, and she reads them as a lack of connection and empathy. You might ask, "But you've been dating Josh for two years! Are you saying you think you're a lesbian?" For you, that is an authentic question, begging for information. For her, it is an indication that you have not been paying any attention.

Your question about Josh also indicates that, like Reagan and Monette, you have yet to learn a key distinction. Gender is separate from sexuality.

Monette's first assumption about Teddy being gay is typical of widespread confusion about sexual orientation and gender. Most of the parents I interviewed shared this confusion when they were first confronted with their child's gender nonconformity. As Monette was well aware, it *is* ridiculous to think about a two-year-old as gay. At the age of two, a child is perhaps a decade away from having any understanding of sexual orientation. However, by the age of two or three most children can clearly state, as Teddy does above, what gender they are. The term *transgender* was also problematic for Monette because she associated it with sexual orientation. Like Monette, most parents are not prepared to consider gender nonconformity beyond the stereotypical concepts of sissy or tomboy. Consider Harry's explanation of his experience with Mickie, the child he had thought of as a tomboy:

> Olivia and I knew that Mickie was different by the time he was three, but trans was not part of our vocabulary until he was a senior in high school. He was very depressed about his body changing. He finally found a therapist that he could speak to and came out to that therapist rather quickly.
>
> From the first moment Mickie could make choices about what to wear, he insisted on no dresses, bows or frills. For example, between the ages of about three to maybe seven, he presented as a male, was very insistent about it and would not be coaxed or ordered into wearing any other kind of outfit. But at his first communion, his mother and I insisted that he wear the traditional white dress with a veil. He did, but he hated it, and on the way home, in the back seat of the car, he took the dress off.
>
> We assumed that we just had a tomboy who was really strong in her conviction to be a tomboy but that at some point this thing would play itself out, and one day I'd be walking my daughter down the aisle in another white dress. Well, Mickie is now in the city and has a heterosexual girlfriend, so it may happen. There may be that other white dress, but Mickie won't be wearing it.

Once Mickie came out as transgender, the predominant emotion for Harry and Olivia was not denial. Instead, Harry reports, "the deepest feeling was loss of our daughter. In fact, she was youngest, and the three older children were boys, so she was our girl." As with denial, the sense of loss is quite prevalent for parents and comes in many forms. Comments such as "you aren't losing a daughter, you're gaining a son" do not necessarily help because there *are* at least parts of the daughter that are gone. A missing part might be something apparently insignificant. For Karen and me it was a nose. Thanks in part to a high school baseball injury back when he was Jared, our kid had a noticeable, but not necessarily prominent, bump on the bridge of his nose. As a guy, that bump just added character to his face, but, upon starting transition, it suddenly gained prominence. After she had the bump removed along with minor alterations to create a more feminine contour, it felt to Karen and me as if something was missing. In a bizarre way, we mourned that bump.

As Ellen, a mother whose son identified as female as a young adult observes, it might be the sound of our child that we miss:

> My only real sadness is the loss of his voice because it's a beautiful voice—not the singing voice, the speaking voice—and I've always loved it. The thought of not having that lovely voice, I would really, really miss it. [Laughing] That's really the only thing I ever cared about. It's amazing what you latch onto.

Not only do we latch onto aspects of our child such as a nose or a voice, we often attach the child to ourselves and others in our lives in complex ways. Another mom, named Janice, lost more than her daughter Glenda during transition. Janice had come out as bisexual when Glenda came out as lesbian at age sixteen. The result was a profound sense of partnership and kinship between them. Later, when Glenda came out as transsexual, Janice felt as if she had lost a soul mate, but she lost even more than that: "her middle name was the same as my grandmother's, so I lost that as well."

Of course, children often become more distant from their parents with age. I remember my dad's response the first time I complained about my college-age kids not staying in touch: "Get used to it. It doesn't get any better as they get older." With a trans child, however, that distance can be magnified exponentially. My father may not hear from me for several weeks, but when I call, he still hears the voice that he remembers cracking during puberty. He can still visualize my face and choice of clothing. His memories of having a catch with me in the back yard still represent father-son bonding. Despite any changes that have occurred over the years, I am still his son.

But with a trans child, it is not just the past that gets lost. Several parents that I interviewed spoke of grieving the loss of future events, of expectations not being realized or dreams being shattered. It could be Harry's vision of walking his daughter down the aisle or a mom's dream of helping her daughter to breastfeed. Of course, these notions of the future may not play out regardless of issues with gender, but when those expectations are suddenly erased for reasons so foreign to our experience, it is easy for parents to feel betrayed. Even when we feel that we have overcome loss, it can still nag at us. One mother, for example, whose adult son had transitioned to female while away from home, sensed during their next visit that this was the same person and that she had not lost her son at all. She noted, however, that she still sometimes struggles "with this vague but powerful sense of loss." So, our child's transition might mean that beyond the loss of certain traits or qualities of our child, we also lose parts of our past, our future, and our connection to family.

Not all responses are so wistful, nor is every child patient with the parental struggle to catch up with the changes that are taking place. In fact, parents of adult children often find out what is happening quite late in the process, and this can create severe tension in the relationship. Iris was taken totally by surprise, and her daughter, Tiffany, offered no time to adapt.

> I became aware when I got a call from her—I'm going to use *her* because now she is my daughter—to come over for a drink. I thought that she and her girlfriend were going to get married. So we sat around and just chit-chatted for a while, when she said, "I have gender identity disorder," and I had no idea what that was, none whatsoever. Tiffany pointed out that she wasn't dressing the same, and it didn't really matter to me if she was more in touch with her feminine side. I thought, "Whatever you do in your house is totally up to you,"
>
> I didn't figure it out until she wouldn't come over. That was odd because we lived only half a mile from each other and the two of us were always extremely close. So, finally we were chatting online one day after I had done some research and realized that, wow, this was kind of serious! I figured she needed to talk to somebody. I said, "This is bigger than you and your girlfriend and us. You

11

really should see someone," only to find out that she already was.

She said that she would not come over again unless she could come dressed as a girl. But we weren't ready for that yet; our whole experience with that was like with Jerry Springer or something negative. We didn't even know if it was real or if it was going to stick.

Looking back, there were hints. When puberty hit, she'd be sick every day at school and have to be picked up. Still, we had no idea. She wasn't feminine, didn't play with girl stuff. She liked to work on cars. I knew she didn't like her body because she wore very baggy clothes. But she wasn't a happy child. It felt like she was struggling with being comfortable with herself.

From the description, it seems clear that Tiffany had been struggling with her gender nonconformity for years, and she desperately needed to move forward, but cutting her family out of the process was hurtful, and Iris was predictably angry. Ironically, Tiffany had sent Iris a birthday card a few weeks earlier that read, "I can talk to you about anything," yet she obviously felt that she couldn't talk about being transgender even though she had been experimenting with living as a woman on weekends for two years. Iris was angry that Tiffany had held this back, especially since the relationship had felt so open to her. She complained about being left completely out of the process until all the decisions had been made—Tiffany was in therapy and was already on hormones. Iris explained it this way: "I was angry that we were already at a point of no return. We were just forced to accept it. We weren't given the time to realize that something was changing. The corner had been turned before we even knew what was going on. It was just, 'Here it is, and, oh, by the way, you won't see me until I can come over dressed as a girl.' We just weren't ready for that."

But some children provide information in even more confrontational ways. I spoke to Rhonda, our next mom, well after she had dealt with pronoun changes as well as her outrage about the way she learned about her child's transsexualism:

I came out as a lesbian twelve years ago, and he had been out as a butch lesbian. It started when I was attending the Gay Pride March in May of '03, and he was marching. He was one of the speakers, and said he was

12

Casey. I really didn't think anything of it. I mean, it could have been an alias.

Then in the fall of '04—he hadn't been living with me at the time—he ended up coming out as a transgender person on the front page of our newspaper in a feature article. I didn't know about it until I got a hysterical call from my daughter, who is three years older than him, saying, "It's awful. Did you see the paper?" In the article he claimed that his mother had thrown him out of the house because he was trans, which was not true. I threw him out because he was being obnoxious to me. It had nothing to do with his being trans. He did not use my name, but still it was clearly me that it was about. We found out about the name change in the probate section of the paper.

From a parent's perspective, it's hard to imagine why a child would make such an accusation, especially in a public forum, but children do not necessarily take such actions out of vindictiveness. I did not speak with Casey, so I can only guess, but his claim about being kicked out may not be the perverse lie that it seems to be to Rhonda. He might have embellished details to feed a reporter a sensational story, but he also might have felt so unaccepted that he lashed out at the safest target, his mother. His obnoxious behavior that got him kicked out of the house may have been prompted by the anxiety he was feeling over gender, and he may have conflated those feelings with being kicked out. In that case, he could actually have believed what was reported in the article to be true.

When a child takes a combative position, the parent can gain needed distance by reciting this mantra: "This is not about me." As much as a betrayal such as Casey's feels like a slap in the face and a blatantly false accusation, it is helpful to remember the stress that the child is facing. Just as it doesn't help to create excuses for our child, it also is doesn't help to invent motives for our child's hurtful actions. If we can keep the door open to further communication and remain open in our interpretation of hostile behavior, we may still be able to heal the relationship and help our child. In this case, despite Casey's rejection of her, Rhonda was able to move beyond her anger with him. The situation and the relationship had improved considerably by the time of our interview. Casey had moved back in and he and Rhonda were getting along well. Furthermore, Rhonda saw Casey as reacting to inflexible cultural norms. She ended our interview with this observation: "I feel very angry that a person could be gender-variant and have to go to such extremes as hormones and surgery to be accepted for who they really are in our society." So Rhonda had managed to move from anger and resentment to empathy with Casey. Her anger and resentment is now directed toward the limitations placed on her child by society's inflexibility and callousness.

Rather than being directed toward the child or the shortcomings of an uninformed culture, however, anger might focus on the other parent. This often happens if the parents disagree about the proper approach to take. One mom reports that she spoke to a therapist who had extensive training in gender-related issues and arranged for the therapist to meet her son, not for a formal session, but simply for the therapist to meet the child. Her husband was furious and remained angry for months. He and his wife had spoken about the situation, and he accepted that homosexuality was not reversible, but he believed that they could control gender identity and expression.

In contrast, anger can sometimes be rather light-hearted. Here are responses from two moms who express rather playful anger:

> Part of me was angry at him, you know, like "Your life would be so easy. Why are you doing this?" And now it's even harder because he's thinking that he's preferring guys, so I'm thinking, "Come on. You could just stay a girl and it would be way easier." Of course, I know now that is not the way it happens, but you want things to be easy for your kid.[6]

and

> I also remember saying I didn't think it was fair to become female and never have to deal with cramps or bleeding, two factors I'd have loved to have avoided.

Anger is a predictable response to a sudden revelation or to being excluded from the process of transition, but fear and worry are also prominent. The parents who stressed these feelings during interviews often had learned about their child's gender issues during the child's teen years. There are two primary concerns here: fear for their child's safety and worry about how others will respond. Both are well founded. Several of the parents confirmed that their child had been assaulted, and almost all of them referred to bullying. Responses of family, friends, and even professional caregivers can be very hurtful. One mom sums it up this way:

> The fear was about how other people would respond to my very sensitive, compassionate kid and not wanting any pain there that was unwarranted. I am still fearful of what could happen out there in the big world, and I don't think that will ever go away. Like Cailin has said, "What would happen if I were arrested? I don't want to be thrown in with the guys." There are all kinds of stories of the police just turning the other way.

Another parent indicates the nagging persistence of the list of concerns.

> We couldn't avoid the topic between ourselves. How on earth could she/we afford this? How would the world perceive her/us? Would our family and friends turn their backs on us? Would she ever be safe, happy, gainfully employed?

Some worries and fears, however, might be less obvious. Some parents worry about the motives of those who are providing information. The Internet offers myriad outlets, but it is a challenge to sort out which information is backed by viable research. One mother from the U.K. was skeptical about the online information that her daughter had been accessing and found herself wondering "whether this is this actually real or an idea gleaned from U.S. web sites." Another couple fretted over whether to allow their son to stay in the "gender cabin" at an LGBT summer camp, entertaining fears that "they would convince him to be trans." Another mom, knowing that her son wants to have a family and to be loved, worries that those wishes might never be realized. She sees relationships being necessarily more difficult and potentially dangerous for her son. Other parents worry that they will slip up with a pronoun and unintentionally disclose their child's status. I also spoke to a mother who is worried because her daughter focuses so much on the fear of being discovered. The mother emphasizes the growing level of general acceptance and all the supportive people in their lives in an effort to move her daughter away from a yes-but-what-if mindset, but she has had limited success.

But that worry is from the perspective of a mother who knows that her child is transsexual. Many parents do not have the luxury of such certainty. A child may exhibit cross-gender behavior, but that does not mean he should be stuffed in the transsexual box. Here's what the mother of an eight-year-old feminine boy has to say:

> I am concerned about puberty for him. I mean, it's always there for me—will he be trans? I'd be blown away—shocked—if that's not the way he wants to go. But I don't do anything to encourage it or discourage it. I just don't know, so I have anxiety when it comes to not knowing what will happen. I know that there is this big conference and part of me wants to go, but I second-guess myself and wonder if he's ready or if I should expose him to that because it may not be who he is. I know that there is a spectrum, and until he shows signs of being distraught or depressed, I think I shouldn't go.

When she says there is a spectrum, she indicates an awareness that, being eight years old, her feminine son is at an age to begin defining himself—to begin considering what kind of box he might find comfortable. If not the boy box, the girl box, the cross-dresser box? Which box? How many boxes are there? When is the right time to decide on a box? *Is* there a right time to decide on a box? This mother's ability to allow her child room to remain unboxed is admirable because she wants clarity, even longs for it, but is consciously willing herself to remain patient. She is lucky to have people around her who have supported her acceptance of uncertainty.

Not everyone has such patience or such support. For some people, the anxiety that accompanies uncertainty is unacceptable, and those who seem to be most certain about their assumptions are often the least informed and the most likely to force the issue. Brent, a trans man in his thirties, was attending a family gathering at his mother's house. Tensions were high, especially with Brent's sister-in-law, who could not make sense of Brent's transition, which was an affront to her world view. For her, Brent's presence as a man posed a threat, and while Brent was using the bathroom, she pounded on the door, screaming for him to release his niece. The niece was in another part of the house, but the sister-in-law had assumed that Brent had taken her into the bathroom to molest her. Such atrocious behavior frays the fabric of a family, and dismissing such a tirade with "that's *her* problem" may ease some of the tension, but it does nothing to mend the family bonds or address the sister-in-law's anxiety. In some cases, unaccepting relatives present a difficult either-or choice for parents. In essence the sister-in-law is asking, "Who is leaving this family, us or that deviant?" Despite such intransigence, the views of even those who are most obstinate sometimes eventually soften with time and patience.

In contrast, some of the most troubling worries end up being groundless. One mom feared the response of her husband, a straight-laced military retiree, and kept him in the dark about their daughter's struggle with gender for two years. When she finally told him, he was visibly shaken and said, "The poor kid. I had no idea!" He then greeted their daughter with a big hug when she arrived home from work and proceeded in the coming weeks not only to find a trans-gender support group but to attend the meetings as well. In speaking about how her husband handled the news, the mom said, "That's the proudest I've ever been of him, and he's done plenty of things that make me proud." After finally confiding in him, she felt sad that she had not trusted him and guilty for holding back so long.

Sadness and guilt may be the most prevalent responses that I encountered throughout interviews. Parents expressed sadness that childhood photographs would now bring pangs of loss or must be put away, that the daughter they had always wanted was being taken away from them, that their child's life would now be more difficult, or that the world will now see their child as a freak rather than wonderful person that they know. One mother was sad that her son had not known that she would be accepting of him. A father of a four-year-old was sad that he would never experience the joy of having a catch with his son in the back yard. More than one mother mentioned sadness over the removal of her daughter's breasts. Beyond this, some parents express sadness about the lack of support that all of them face, such as this mom:

> It is a very difficult and silent topic. There is very little information and it is crucial for us as parents to educate

ourselves to be able to help and support our transgender children. It is sad to see that for parents there is hardly any support, especially for parents of very young children, and they have to face custody battles, doctors, and the fear of losing their children.

Guilt is also quite common for a parent who deals with a gender-nonconforming child. Parents often feel guilty that they should have noticed what was happening earlier. Regardless of when parents learn what is going on, there is plenty of room for guilt. When I asked what prompted her guilt, one mother quipped "I was raised Catholic." After a hearty laugh, she went on, "What kind of mom was I that I didn't catch this?" But catching it early does not clear away the potential for guilt; it just opens the door to a different strain: "How do we do this the right way and not mess up our kid?" There is no end to the possible reasons for parents to assume blame. Many parents wonder if they somehow unwittingly caused the problem. Here are three samples:

I thought, does this mean I screwed my kid up somehow? His dad and I struggled when he was young. Did that stress him out because it was not always easy for us? Does it mean that I am not a normal mom? There is this theory that stress during pregnancy could affect things. I was really stressed. Our marriage was not going well at all during my pregnancy, but I don't know if there is any real truth to that.

Here's a child that is defective and what did I do to create it. Is it something in my genes? In my husband's genes? If I hadn't smoked when I was pregnant, would this not have happened?

When I was pregnant, I miscarried his other twin, then I was at party and I drank because I didn't know he was still there. We didn't want a boy; we wanted another girl. And this is really magical thinking, but I thought, "I wonder if my power of thought was so strong that I created this?" which is ridiculous, but, you know, you think everything.

All three of these quotations are from mothers, which is not to say that fathers feel no guilt, but it is mothers who have traditionally borne the blame for their children's' faults. Starting with Freud's conclusion in 1910 that Leonardo da Vinci's mother deprived him of fatherly influence, and prominent at least since psychiatrist Leo Kanner's "refrigerator mother" theory in the 1940s, the pathological mother has been recognized as the cause for everything from autism to homosexuality. Domineering mothers are still seen as a significant factor in gender dysphoria by some psychologists.[7] Almost every one of the mothers that I spoke to has experienced guilt, and many of them have pondered if they have somehow caused the problem.

Regardless of the choices a parent makes, hindsight can always find a way of pointing its finger. Instead of purposely discouraging cross-gender behavior, some parents have ignored it, hoping that it would go away. In retrospect those parents express guilt that they failed to offer the nurturance that the child deserved. But parents face a damned-if-you-do-damned-if-you-don't dilemma. No matter what parenting decisions they make, somebody, whether it be themselves, their child or others, can always second-guess those decisions if they are deemed to produce subpar results—and both gender nonconformity and transsexualism are certainly considered subpar. This no-win situation is summed up by Tracie, who became aware of her son's transsexual status when he was twenty-six.

> Unfortunately we were late to the table in terms of helping him, and his take on what we did as parents is a bit different than ours. He does know we love him, but he feels like we put way more pressure on him to be a girl (his birth gender) than we think we did. We bought him trucks (and bought both him and his older brother dolls) and in general let him dress as he pleased, but we also hoped he would occasionally dress like the girl we thought he was. It really did not occur to us that there was a real alternative, but hindsight brings doubt, so we have guilt.

Although there are common threads and shared emotions in the stories of these families, there are no absolutes. Parents learn of issues in a variety of ways and their children begin to chafe at the restraints of gender at a variety of ages. Some children provide clear indications of discomfort from the time that they can express themselves, but others do not realize what is going on until adulthood. Invariably, the parents can look back and see hints of gender nonconformity in childhood, but in some cases there are few if any such hints. For Karen and me, there was no real indication. Until Cadence announced that she was transsexual at age twenty-three, we had assumed that she might be gay, but until that moment our perception was that she was clearly male.

For the sake of clarity, I will switch to male pronouns as I explore her history. As a child, he was exceptionally verbal, speaking in full sentences by age one, in highly complex sentences before age three, and reading fluently before age five. He never asked for dolls or played with them while with girls. He was never macho but also was certainly not feminine and never cross-dressed. He excelled in baseball and basketball, playing at the varsity level in both for all four years of high school. The only hints from childhood were that his friendships were primarily with girls until reaching school age and that he preferred to pee while sitting. That's it.

I have interviewed other parents who had similar experiences with children who came out as transgender as late as in their forties. For example, Tammy found out that her forty-two-year-old son was trans when his wife abandoned him after discovering women's clothing in his closet. Tammy was completely surprised, and, upon reflection, could recall only two very vague hints from his childhood: he had trouble making friends and he always wore shirts when in the sun.

Another mother, Lana, had raised her daughter Lydia as a girl and had wondered if she was a lesbian when she was in high school, but Lydia denied it. As a young girl, Lydia was not interested in dolls and idolized her older brother, even wanting to be a boy scout, but she was not a tomboy. She remembers thinking at age five or six that she would rather have been a boy, but she wore dresses throughout high school, and if anyone had suggested that she was transgender at that time, Lydia would have laughed at them. Yet when she was twenty-five, she sent Lana a long letter with a large packet of information in which she explained that she was now Nathan, was taking testosterone and had been living as a man for a year.

As explained by another mother, Shanon, there are also situations in which the messages we receive are even more mixed:

In the baby group, most of the babies were girls. I noticed by age one or two that the others had a coy kind of behavior, but Daphne did not. I thought, "Well, she's just more serious." By four, it was starting to get hard to get her into a dress, and by age five, phases like Spider-man and Batman came in. She had to wear her Spider-man suit every day. In fact, one of the incidents where we thought something might be up was a Halloween party at school when all the boys wore their Spiderman suits and all the girls were fairy princesses. Well, she got teased by both the boys and girls because she went as Spiderman. She had worn the suit out, so I had bought her another one to wear a few days later on Halloween night, but she threw it in the trash. That was the end of that.

I didn't know what transgender was; I just assumed that she'd be a lesbian. It was my mom who mentioned tomboy, and Daphne said, "Yeah, that's what I am." That worked for a little while, but by age eight things were becoming emotionally critical. I knew something was up; I just had no idea what. But my situation is not like other parents who say, "Oh, I knew by age two or three that he was really a boy." In fact, I can even remember being glad that I had a feminine girl, thinking "Ugh, those boys that I see. I'm so glad I don't have one of those."

He still is not rough and tumble; he's more like a sci-ence nerd. He's quite effeminate, but then so is my hus-band. That's just his nature. So, even tomboy was not fitting for me. Then I saw a show on intersex[8] and I won-dered if it might be something like that, so I checked records, but there was nothing odd about the amnio before birth, and tests show two X chromosomes. When he was eight or nine, I saw a show on transgender. I thought, "Oh, my God. I wonder if that's what is going on."

At that time there were a lot of bedtime discus-sions, a lot of anxiety at night—often until midnight—with her crying, "I don't know what's wrong with me. I don't feel right." I didn't know what to say. I didn't even have a label for it but tried to assure her with "there are many ways of being a girl. I have friends who are lesbians. Look at this one. She's a house painter, and that one is a dog trainer." That did not seem to placate her.

With Daphne's varied responses and behaviors, who could possibly predict the outcome? Even if Shanon had possessed the vocabulary that allowed her to label what was happening, it is unlikely that she could sort out everything that was at play, and it is even more unlikely that anything she said could assuage a nine-year-old child's sense of isolation. Certainly the roles she offered as possible choices for lesbians were of no help.

So, how do we sort out a child's gender-driven trauma? Perhaps the most important key for parents is to gain more complete knowledge of the experience that their child is encountering. Some gain that knowledge through reading, others through viewing documentary films or television programs, some by reaching out to support groups such as PFLAG, and still others by meeting and interacting with gender-nonconforming and transsexual people. With additional knowledge, gender nonconformity can become less alien and threatening.

We can start by at least expanding our thinking, by moving away from the vehement simplicity of "I know you're a boy" toward the contingent complexity of "I'm not sure what's going on." It is possible that by learning new vocabulary so that she has a few additional boxes for sorting, Shanon can gain a more accurate understanding of what is happening with Daphne. If she can open herself to embrace a rainbow of possibilities rather than to stay trapped in the dualism of pink and blue,[9] she has a chance of helping Daphne climb out of her thorny box so that together they can consider what is possible. Rather than judging Daphne or fearing the judgments others are making of her, Shanon can work with Daphne to better judge how to proceed.

CHAPTER 2

Coming Out/Staying In

"Who do I tell, and how do I tell them?"
"What do I say? When do I say it?"
"What will they say? How will I deal with that?"

W E ALL FRET OVER SUCH questions as those above and a host of others. Nobody gets through this ordeal alone, and you can certainly use the support of others to sort out everything that you will now have to confront. Yet, if you are like most of the parents that I have interviewed, you dread reaching out for that support because there is no assurance that it will be there. Not knowing what to expect from others, we often envision the worst possible response, and the longer we hold that vision, the more it feels inevitable. Since we dread facing that inevitable outcome, we hold back, allowing that vision to fester. It's not unusual to be leery of sharing the information, even with a spouse.

Congratulations, you are now in the closet! Sort of feels like that box in the last chapter, doesn't it? As uncomfortable as it feels, being in this box helps us to understand how our child has felt, perhaps for years or even decades, prior to climbing out and letting us know who she is and what her life has been. Leslie Feinberg, one of the trans community's most vocal advocates offers a profound insight into the level of trust it has taken for our child to come out to us, especially if the child was anxious enough to put off coming out for an extended time. Although that delay may feel like a betrayal to us, Feinberg asks that we consider the amount of love and trust it takes to come forward despite the gut-wrenching fear of being rejected and losing us.[10] That may seem melodramatic, but the fear of being disowned and abandoned is very real for a gender-nonconforming child, regardless of how old the child is or how open and strong a parent may assume the relationship to be, and research has revealed high levels of anxiety and excessive rates of suicidal thoughts and actions in the trans community.[11]

Of course, it is possible that, instead of through disclosure, you found out about your child's situation through discovery, either by accident or design. Regardless of how you learned about it, you have cause to celebrate because you now have an opportunity to help provide your child with support that has not been previously available. So the fact that your child is now out of the box and you are stuffed into it is good news despite how it feels at the moment.

Fortunately, you get to choose how to proceed and there are plenty of options to exercise. You can try to stay in the closet and keep this all to yourself, working to hide it from everyone. You can open the door a crack, allowing a therapist in with the hope of gaining perspective and solace. You can open it a bit further and share your situation with your spouse or a few trusted family members and friends, which would certainly be cheaper than the therapist but also would carry more risk. You could combine those two choices, having the therapist help you figure out who else you can come out to. You might even fling the door wide open and share candidly with others to find out who will offer support and who will not.[12]

You may feel the need to put off telling anyone until you can answer all the questions that may be asked. Yes, you need information, but you don't have to have everything fully researched prior to opening up to your spouse, your closest friends, or your immediate family. These people may be helpful to you, and there is no rule that states you must be a martyr, holding this in and "protecting" your child. In reaching out for support, you may find that some people in your life give you access to information you thought you needed to have before speaking to them.

There are, however, effective and ineffective ways of coming out. The trick is to come out the right amount to the right person at the right time. Keep in mind that the information that you are divulging is likely to be hard for others to process and even harder to accept. It won't work to unload every detail of your child's situation along with all your misgivings and confusion. So, let's explore what it means to come out successfully.

To begin, it's worthwhile to examine your own mental state by asking yourself several questions. How strong or vulnerable do you feel? How strong are your relationships with the people in your life? How well can you stand up to discrimination and disapproval? How well can you keep a secret and evade or even lie to cover it up if you need to? The answers to those questions will help you consider how to proceed.

Let's assess the situation in terms of assets and liabilities: what might you gain or lose by coming out with your news to others?

Reasons to Stay in Your Closet
- Rejection, anger, and gossip
- Loss of relationship
- Misunderstandings
- Creating a negative impression
- Loss of control
- Psychological and emotional stress
- Compromising your child's privacy

Reasons to Come Out of Your Closet
- Catharsis: relief from sharing the burden
- Physical and psychological health
- Support and help
- Self-validation/gaining insight
- Self-defense
- Moral obligation
- Social influence
- Self-awareness
- Freedom to live a more authentic life
- Personal empowerment—offering testimony to confront stigma or discrimination

Although some of the above points are self-explanatory, others require elaboration. Since the fear of other people's responses tends to be the most prominent block for newly boxed-in parents, let's take a look at it first. Fear of rejection or anger can provoke significant delays, and it might be the key factor that causes people to put off coming out to their spouse. That was certainly the case for the mom at the end of chapter one whose husband was retired from the military. Clearly, though, she had misread him, and it is possible for you to misread your spouse's response as well. So, if you are reading this before coming out to your spouse, it might be worthwhile to take stock of the situation by considering the discussion below rather than simply blurting it out. Although holding back may feel like a betrayal, it might also make a significant positive difference in the outcome. Unfortunately, there are no guarantees, and you can't control how anyone will respond; you can, however, control how you proceed.

In fact, fear of rejection is the reason that I put off coming out to my family. "Knowing" that my parents and siblings are more conservative than I am, I avoided saying anything about Cadence to them for three years despite Karen's prompting me to open up. I realized that I was experiencing the same anxiety that Cadence had gone through before coming out to us; yet, for me, *her* fear was illogical because she should have known that we would never disown her, but *my* fear was reasonable because . . .

I did not have a valid reason, but that did not stop me from believing that my fear was well grounded.

In hindsight, I realize how prejudiced I was being. I was assuming that my parents and siblings would not be able to accept my revelation because I "knew" that transsexualism would be an affront to their religion and because they have had very little exposure to the LGBTQ community. In my arrogance, I had even managed to convince myself that I was protecting them from hurtful information. I thought that they might be able to accept Cadence if she were merely gay, but trans? No way! The longer I allowed myself to breathe life into those assumptions, the more certain I became that they were accurate, the more "real" they seemed and the more I feared losing my family. I had the benefit of distance, living an eleven-hour drive away, so I steeped in this stew of illusions for three years.

My hand was finally forced when the family was going to get together, so I had no choice but to come forward. Carefully considering my options, I chose to come out first to my younger sister. She had always been empathic in the past, and she was the one who I considered most likely to be open to my revelation. I rehearsed what I would say, starting by explaining that we would need her support for something that might be hard to understand. Swallowing hard, I called and was relieved when she was totally accepting from the moment I explained our situation. Of course, at the end of the call, she ruined my relief by asking, "So, when are you telling Mom and Dad?" I said that I wasn't sure, hoping that I could stall indefinitely, but she turned up the heat with, "Well, do it soon, because I can't sit on this for long."

So much for support! I found myself thinking, "Great! Now I've done it!"

I had reached the point of no return. Even then, I put off calling my parents for another week, dreading the day that I'd find the courage to pick up the phone. When I finally made the call, there was no issue. Both of my parents were immediately accepting. My mother's first response was, "I want pictures." She wanted to know what her grandchild would look like throughout the transition. Even more amazing, she switched to female pronouns and to Cadence rather than Jared in the same conversation. It's possible that she has slid back while out of my earshot, but, to this day, I have never heard her slip.

Emboldened by this response and despite my trepidation, I called my older sister then my younger brother. Their response was almost verbatim, "Let Cadence know that there is all the love and support in the world, right here." It was almost as if they had spoken to each other before I called to rehearse what they would say. I had wallowed in fear for three years for nothing. In retrospect, there had been plenty of evidence that I had nothing to fear. My family had always been loving and had never given me any reason to expect that they would abandon me or my child.

Karen was much more open than I was. Karen lost her mother to cancer in the early 1980s, so the first family member that she spoke to was her aunt, her mother's twin sister. Her aunt was not only accepting and supportive, she also shared that one of the nurses at her dialysis clinic was a trans man. Next Karen came out to her younger brother, who has three children. She and her brother are quite close, and he was also quite accepting when Karen spoke to him. She left it to him to share the information with his children.

We had concerns, however about speaking to Karen's father because, at the time that Cadence came out, Karen's stepmother was going through significant long-term health issues. Having weathered the loss of Karen's mom, her dad was now dealing with the rapid decline of his second wife—negotiating multiple doctors' appointments, health insurance reimbursement delays, and physical therapy sessions as well as handling all meals and household chores. We decided that he had enough emotional stress in his life and that we should hold off. A year later, however, he was set to fly in for a visit, so we had to speak to him. We could not, however, wait until he arrived because our work schedules dictated that the person picking him up at the airport had to be Cadence. So Karen put in a call to him, using essentially the same approach that I would finally use later with my family: we need your support with an issue that may be difficult to understand and accept. His primary concern was about Cadence's safety. He explained by relating an incident that occurred while he was attending Duke University just before World War II. While he was out with friends, they encountered a young man who was a homosexual, and few of his friends roughed the young man up. He could never understand why they did that. The young man had done nothing to them.

Certainly, Karen and I did not have difficult coming out experiences, but not everyone is as fortunate. Others have, indeed, been rejected and become estranged from family members. Some find the strength to dismiss rejection and put it into perspective. For example, Millie, who met resistance from an older sister, simply laid out what she was and was not going to accept, saying, "Look, Jack is a *he*, and I accept him and love him just like he is. You are either going to get on board or you are not. This is the way it is. It's up to you." This retort was adequate for *that* sister, who is now accepting. Another sister, however, does not accept the transition and insists upon using female pronouns. Although Millie confronts her each time it happens, she holds out little hope of the sister coming around, noting that the same sister refuses to accept her own son who is gay. Not everyone is as assertive as Millie and other parents have found the rejection of family more difficult to accept. One mother had always felt very close to her brother and his wife and children, but the brother was not accepting, and they remain estranged to this day.

It is possible, however, to have a situation turn out well even if at first it seems impossible. Ursula's trans daughter showed overt signs of femininity from as early as eighteen months, and the situation early on could not have been much worse.

One acquaintance, who did not take the time to talk to us and understand, sent a rather nasty email to numerous other families in our school which resulted in one of the families contacting the media. The injection of the media into an already stressful situation made things much harder on our family and our child. It's funny though—our experience of our community now is that it is much more friendly than it ever was. Those that were hostile and upset simply avoid us. We have never been confronted by anyone. Much of the rest of the community is very compassionate and goes out of their way to make our child and our family feel welcome and accepted, and many more people say hello to us when we walk to school than ever before.

Even when we think we are coming out in a safe environment, the process may turn out much differently than we expect. Jeanine faced lack of control, misunderstanding, creation of negative impressions and psychological stress all from one incident. She had close friends at work and felt as if she were holding out on them. Hoping that she might be able to create a support network among her colleagues, she came out about her trans son to a co-worker. She had weighed her options carefully and thought that the disclosure would be low-risk because she was pretty sure that the co-worker would be sympathetic. He was, but he shared what she had said with another colleague and the news quickly spread through the entire office, the result being that Jeanine's boss found out about her situation through the rumor mill and was not pleased. He claimed that the response to the office gossip was affecting productivity and eroding morale, but Jeanine later discovered that he was actually angry for personal reasons. He had been very open with the entire staff about having a gay son, and he felt betrayed when she had not come out to him directly. The atmosphere at the office became oppressive enough that Jeanine started to look for another job. She eventually reconciled with her boss and ended up with the network of support that she had originally hoped to create but only after living through months of stress at the office as well as at home. The psychological stress that Jeanine faced as a result of her coming out is unfortunately common,[13] and once we let the cat out the bag, we can't stuff it back in. No one wants to be the subject of a gossip mill. Even worse, we don't want to be pitied, which can feel even more belittling. So it is worthwhile to weigh the consequences of coming out prior to divulging details.

Of course, unburdening yourself may feel good, but simply sharing your burden in the hope that it will make you feel better may backfire as it did for Jeanine.[14] If she had taken two actions, she could have saved herself all the anxiety and distress. First she could have made it clear to her co-worker that she was speaking in confidence. We often assume that this is understood, but the situation called for more caution. In fact, she could have enlisted her co-working in helping her to plan a strategy—working as a team to decide who should be told next. It's possible that in doing that, they would have realized that their supervisor needed to be next in line to hear the news. Second, it clearly would have been to her benefit to come out to her boss first rather than her co-worker. Even if she feared that her boss might take the news poorly, it would have been better for her to personally reveal the situation rather than having it done by someone else. Although in this instance, her colleague was not purposely undermining her, not all work cultures are supportive and there are plenty of situations in which a colleague could purposely use information against you. Let's face it—the revelation that you have a trans child has the potential to create an uproar. So you should definitely see to it that it is you who shares details of your situation if you are concerned that someone else might reveal those details in an effort to discredit you. It is better that you should share sensitive information rather than allowing someone else to do so because doing so allows you to provide the information in the most productive context.[15]

All the parents that I have spoken to want to hear from someone that they are doing the right thing for their child, so it is unlikely that we can cope well if we share our experience with nobody. To receive the support and help of others we need to let them know what we are facing. Let's say you are talking with a friend you have not seen for six months, the same six months that you've been dealing with your eight-year-old daughter's insistence that she be called Stevie, not Stephanie. How likely is it that, with no prompting from you, your friend will blurt out, "Let me tell you about an incredible conversation that I had yesterday with Margie Johnson—you know Margie, don't you? Well, her son is transgender. You know what that means, right? He thinks he's a girl! Anyway, Margie is working to put together a group for families who have the same problem. She made it sound like it was no big deal, that all the parents need is the support of others to deal with the whole thing. I think my sister could use that group because Ginny has been refusing to wear girls' underwear for about a year now."

It would be wonderful to have such a clairvoyant friend, but rather than waiting for her to show up and blurt out information that might help us, we stand a much better chance of getting that information if we open our closet door to let a friend know that we are looking for support. For example, there was no way for me to realize that my family was supportive until I came out to them. When I finally did so, when my fears had proved to be groundless, and when my guilt for not trusting them had dissipated, I experienced an incredible rush of relief—even euphoria. I felt confirmed, loved, and supported—buoyant. To this day, when thinking back to that moment, the tears well in my eyes.

Furthermore, it is by coming out to others that Karen and I were directed to friends who were having experiences similar to ours, and we found out about several of the sources referred to in this book because we took the risk of revealing our situation to others who just happened to have useful information for us. Two examples come to mind. When Karen and I came out to the pastor of our former church, he said, "You know Bob and Cheryl are dealing with the same thing. Gretchen transitioned last year." We had sung with Bob and Cheryl in the church choir years earlier and had fallen out of touch. During conversation with another couple who sang with us at a different church, decades earlier, we asked how Leslie, their younger daughter was doing. The answer was, "Well, it's interesting that your ask. Leslie is now Lee." Of course, both of these revelations resulted in lengthy conversations with shared travails and concerns. The result is that Karen and I joke that we have unearthed a previously unconsidered possible cause of transsexualism: excessive in utero exposure to Congregational anthems.

It is possible that coming out may also improve psychological and physical health, especially if we are experiencing anxiety and depression while keeping the secret. Studies have shown that people who hold back information have more headaches, back pain and nausea than those who open up.[16] Anita Kelly, who teaches at the University of Notre Dame, has explored the effects of self-disclosure on physical and psychological health for over a decade. Her findings indicate that there are health benefits from disclosing to a person who we believe to be accepting and supportive—specific benefits being fewer colds, pains, and gastronomic upsets.[17]

Beyond issues of health, it may be necessary to come out in order to protect yourself or your family. If you live in the District of Columbia or one of the small but growing number of states that includes gender expression in its hate crime or employment nondiscrimination laws,[18] it is in your child's best interest to open up to enough people to assure that you have clearly established your child's issues with gender.

In addition, it is in the best interest of your family to come out to key players in your family's life simply because they have a right to know what is happening, even if you believe that holding back will protect them from anxiety or hurt. The disrespect that I showed my family is just one example of this. Luckily for me, my family was forgiving. A more compelling example is provided by Reagan and Lloyd, who worked with their fourteen-year-old transgender child to conceal the issue from their younger son, Franklin, who was eleven. Assuming that they were saving Franklin from hurt, embarrassment and potential harassment from peers, they conspired for months to keep him in the dark. Despite their efforts, he was well aware that something was up and finally confronted them, asking, "What's wrong with Edison? He's got cancer or something, hasn't he? He's dying, and you are not telling me. I'd rather know." Although their intention was to protect Franklin, Reagan and Lloyd had brought him anguish and undermined his trust in them. Franklin had read their hesitation to share the situation with him as deception and lies.

Many of the parents that I have interviewed are open about their trans child simply because they want others to be more aware and accepting of gender-nonconforming people. The reasoning here, is that by staying in the closet, we allow others to think that there is something wrong, reprehensible, degrading or "dirty" about gender nonconformity or transsexuality. The more we come out, the more we work to normalize gender nonconformity and help others to accept variations from the narrow binary restrictions that are assumed to be the norm. Many parents, Karen and I included, purposely speak about our trans child to create conversations in which people hear about our child and the normalcy of her life—the daily trials and triumphs that she has in common with others, whether they be personal or work-related. Of course, there is also a benefit in speaking of the special challenges she faces as a trans woman and that our family faces in supporting her. We can move the global conversation about gender forward only if we generate our part of that conversation. If, instead, we hold back to conceal our situation, we promote the widely held assumption that gender nonconformity deserves to be kept in the shadows, hidden away with other dark secrets.

If nothing else, by coming out to someone, we offer them the possibility of making a choice. They might respond supportively or not, but if we never tell them, we deprive them of the opportunity to choose freely how they will respond. This was certainly true of my family and of Karen's father. Until we told them what was happening, they had no opportunity to provide support.

Test Driving the Coming Out Process

Who needs to know? One way to sort this out is to consider who is closest to you and your child and who might be most hurt by be being left out of the loop. Who has an ongoing relationship and spends time with you and your child? Who has offered support in the past and shown concern for your family? Here's a useful question to ask yourself: Do I feel as if I am betraying her by keeping this a secret? If the answer is yes, you need to consider how your might come out to that person.

Like driving a car, we get better at the coming out process with practice. The first time out you are likely to be clumsy and lack control, so there is no point in starting off in heavy traffic. You need to pick an environment that will help you to gain proficiency. The action that you are taking is challenging by nature, so there is no need to add to the risk you are taking by starting with someone who has provided ample evidence of being rigid and unaccepting. That person is a busy street in New York City at nine o'clock on a snowy Monday morning. You can't predict what might happen next or what maneuver you'll have to pull off. That is not the place to choose for your first day behind the wheel. Instead, choose someone like my younger sister, a quiet country road with no traffic.

Okay, you've chosen who you will come out to. You're going to speak to your quiet-country-road sister. It helps to plan ahead by rehearsing what to say and how to respond to anticipated questions.

Who might be your best driving instructor—your child, your spouse, a therapist, a pastor or an online support group? Find someone who is willing to offer some help.

Next, plan when you will have this conversation. The information that you are sharing is not something to be dropped into a casual conversation. Instead, let your sister know that you need to speak with her and that it needs to happen when you both have time to explore what comes up.

So, the time has come. Where do you start?[19]

With yourself.

Explain what you need from her authentically. Your first words might be something like, "I need your support with a tough problem," or "You have always been supportive and loving, and that means the world to me," or "I'm not sure where to start because this is really difficult for me" or "Even though I trust you and know that you love me, I'm nervous and worried about sharing this."

It's best to stick to basics rather than to go on about details. Provide the background by explaining what is going on and how you feel. Then explain what you need.

Remember that this is a conversation, a two-way process. Although you are coming to her for support, she will need your support as well. What you are revealing is as much a challenge for her to hear as it is for you to say. Reflect on your response when your child came out to you. Your sister's response won't be identical, but she is likely to experience some of the same emotions. She will ask questions that you may not have answers for. Those questions may come across as unexpected potholes on this first drive, but it won't help to think of those questions as challenges. It's not as if she saw you coming and dug those potholes just to make your test drive difficult.

This is not the time to pretend you know more than you do. If you don't have an answer to a question, simply acknowledge that you don't know. If a question seems confrontational, remember that this moment is just as much about helping her to deal with her response as it is about getting her support. How can you expect her to support you if you can't help her to grapple with your news? Remind yourself that she is confronting her confusion and discomfort, not you. It might help to reassure her that your child is the same lovable kid that you have both cherished and enjoyed, and that who your child is and who you are have not changed.

Despite how you present the information, it is likely to trigger strong emotions. If you have held off coming out to her, she may feel betrayed, wondering why you have hidden this from her. If so, apologize and explain the struggle you have been through in coming to this point. Give her time to absorb what you have to share, and don't expect her to come to grips with it in a single conversation.

Finally, don't assume that you are reading her accurately. This is likely to be one of the most startling revelations that she has experienced, and her initial reaction may be very easy to misunderstand, especially if you enter the conversation with expectations of a particular response. Yes, you know her quite well, and you may well be able to predict her actions in any number of situations, but she may be very disturbed by what you share, and she may find it hard to accept. You won't be able to help her cope with her reaction if you go into the conversation prepared to accept only one response.

You will be in a heightened emotional state, so don't "trust your instincts." If she seems disinterested or distant to you, remind yourself that the way that she *seems* is influenced by what you are feeling at the moment. You cannot *know* what she is experiencing. You can only guess. She may just be trying to process what you are sharing and be unsure how to respond.

It may help to point out the level of fear your child has had to overcome in order to share the dilemma with you, how hard you are working to provide love, support and acceptance, and how your conversation with her is part of that process. During the conversation, find out how much she wants to know and assure her that you will work to give her any information that you don't have at present. If you have information, this is probably not the time to dump it all on her. Just tell her what has happened and how you and your child are coping then let her tell you what else she needs to know.

Once you have finished your test drive, assess how you performed. Did you stay in control of your emotions? Did you approach her in a way that helped her to understand and accept your situation? Did you allow her to respond freely without boxing her in with your expectations? Did you avoid barraging her with unneeded information? It might be worthwhile to share your observations about your test drive with whoever helped you to prepare for this drive. With careful ongoing assessment of your performance, you can become a much better driver, eventually gaining the skill and prowess to negotiate heavy traffic.

Notice that our assessment in the last paragraph examined how you performed as you were coming out, not how your sister responded. Although it is certainly true that you will have to deal with the way that people respond, ultimately all that is in your control is how you handle the process. The guidelines above can help you to avoid mistakes that others have made in coming out, but you will need to find your own way with the process. Some of us prefer a straightforward, here-are-the-facts manner, others a more subdued approach. Whatever your preference, you will have more success if you focus your attention on the person you are coming out to. Just as you learn to adapt your manner of driving to traffic and weather, you can learn to adapt your manner of coming out to individual people. If possible, leave the rush-hour-in-heavy-snow people of your life until you've gained some experience.

Regardless of who you decide to come out to, you need to weigh the potential risks and benefits of doing so because your decision is complicated by the fact that you are revealing something about your child, not yourself, and your child is likely to have strong feelings about how broadly to come out and to whom. Once a transsexual has enough information to know that he is not alone, it is not unusual for him to be eager to complete transition and to come out broadly early in the process,[20] often well before you and other family members are ready. At this point, especially, he will be vulnerable and hungry for acceptance,[21] and he may need help to gain perspective about what is feasible. He is likely to need your support in negotiating this process.

Alternatively, it is possible that you need to come out to people even though he feels strongly that they should not know. Keep in mind that you may need to discuss your coming out with your child for each person that you intend to speak to because your coming out exposes your child in ways that his being gay or lesbian would not. Being out as trans is different than being out as gay or lesbian for at least two reasons. First, when compared to the plight of trans people, it is relatively easy for gays and lesbians to find networks of support through LGBT community centers and in high school and college gay-straight alliance clubs. Although support is far from universal and is dependent not only upon location but also upon family and community dynamics, the LGBT centers and gay-straight alliances that I know of are very supportive of trans people. In contrast, it is still a daunting challenge for trans people to find others who share their identity.[22] Second, gays and lesbians can choose to remain partially closeted—out in some parts of their lives but not in others—and they do not openly announce their variance from "normal" when they are in a public setting. For a trans person, being partially out creates a unique problem.

Imagine that you are the supportive and accepting mother of Peg, a trans woman, who just finished college and has moved back in with you to save money for her transition. To retain her job, Peg needs to be unmistakably male at work, so she wears pants, an oxford cloth shirt and a tie—her straight closet. She wears long sleeves year-round and never roles them up because her shaved arms might prompt questions. To appease her father she is only partially out at home, so she wears women's slacks, a blouse, and perhaps a necklace—her compromise closet. She toys with female mannerisms but wears only light makeup and tones down feminine gestures. She is, however, most comfortable when she is with her trans friends, and on these occasions, she is in a dress, heels, a wig, rings and an ankle bracelet—her favorite closet. Here, she is in full makeup and plays with overtly feminine gestures and mannerisms. Although expensive, she stocks all three closets; although burdensome, she keeps all three organized and sorted; although challenging, she manages to keep gestures, posture and body movements sorted and in place. She has worked hard to maintain all three gender expressions flawlessly, but Peg learns that you have come out about her to your chatty hair dresser and informs you that her boss goes to the same chatty hair dresser. Has her cover been blown? You can't know for sure, but your daughter's job may suddenly be at risk.[23]

This cautionary tale is not meant to suggest that there is nobody that you can come out to safely. The point is to consider possible ramifications and to assure that, regardless of age, your child is aware of who you are sharing information with. The key is to maintain open communication with your child to avoid surprises and to negotiate the coming out process as a unified team.

CHAPTER 3

Coming to Terms with Terms

"I didn't even have a label for it."
"I didn't know what transgender was."
"I didn't understand the difference between sex and gender."

G IVEN THE WAY THAT OUR thinking tends to be boxed in around gender and sexuality, the statements above are quite common when we first encounter gender nonconformity in our children. For a start, let's differentiate the concepts of gender and sex: sex is determined by biology and gender is determined by culture. In our culture, and most others, people think of men and women as opposite sexes and of male and female as opposite genders: you're a man or a woman; you're male or female. We don't consider that you might be something between or a mix of the two. Although those assumptions are an oversimplification, let's accept them for now. The table below provides six areas that will help to tease out the difference between sex and gender.[24] As we work through them, we will consider each row on the chart as a continuum. It helps to think of each row as a playground teeter-totter with the fulcrum in the center. A person might be located at any position along the teeter-totter, not just on the far ends.

At birth, the doctor takes a look at the baby's genitals and, based upon comparison to other babies s/he has examined, proclaims the child's **natal sex**:[25] boy or girl. We assume this declaration to be accurate, but the proclamation (and the sex that is entered on the birth

Male	←Natal Sex→	Female
Male	←Gender Roles →	Female
Male	←Gender Identity →	Female
Male	←Gender Expression →	Female
Male	←Gender Attribution →	Female
Male	←Sexual Orientation →	Female

certificate) is based upon inference, not fact. It is possible for an inter-sex person to be one sex biologically but to live an entire lifetime as the other sex. People come into the world in all varieties, and it in not unusual for a person to have a mix of features that vary from what we accept as the "normal" XX-female and XY-male. A careful look at studies regarding prevalence of intersex births shows that they account for a little under 2% of births world-wide.[26] A full discussion of this issue is outside the purpose of this chapter, but extensive infor-mation is available on the web site for the Intersex Society of North America.[27]

Gender Identity is the self-concept in relation to gender—not just who you think you are, but who you think you are as a man or a woman. Of course, we don't create this image of ourselves in a vac-uum. We can only define ourselves through consideration of the **gen-der roles** that our society assigns to masculinity and femininity. We determine how masculine or feminine we are in comparison to the roles we see others portray. A young boy sees a multitude of men play-ing out their role and considers how he fits into the ways he sees mas-culinity portrayed: a cowboy with pointed boots and a Stetson hat, who talks very little and takes aggressive strides as he walks; a lawyer in a business suit, a tie and tasseled dress shoes, who talks continu-ously and moves very deliberately; a barefoot dancer in tights, who seems to be mute but leaps and prances with amazing athleticism. The list is endless, but without anyone providing specific instructions about the choices he is to make, the boy learns that he is supposed to figure out how he fits into this scheme, what his role is within the constraints of gender as suggested by the examples he is exposed to.

Regardless of how much the boy's parents might intend to provide an open list of possible identities, the child's exposure to media narrows his focus. Mass media of all formats send a clear message: successful girls pay attention to their looks and the relationships in their lives, successful boys are athletic and competitive. Advertisements, books, movies and television programming promote a simple dolls-or-balls paradigm: female identity is marked by playing with dolls and engaging in housekeeping role-play, whereas masculine identity is marked by playing with balls and engaging in contact sports. Girls enjoy looking beautiful and boys enjoy looking strong: boys over there and girls over here. The message is clear: don't cross the line.

Our cultural barriers are not as stringent as they once were, at least for girls, who are often encouraged to engage in team sports.[28] Thanks to Title IX, one of the hard-won advances gained by American feminists, it is permissible for a girl to be quite athletic yet also be considered acceptably feminine. For boys, though, the expectations are much more ironclad. If a boy enjoys playing with a doll, it had better be a male action figure that encourages aggressive, even destructive, role-play. Parents who actively work to broaden their family's definition of gender roles are likely to have limited success in downplaying the divisions dictated by the larger culture. Even if Daddy does all of the cooking and Mommy makes most of the money, exposure to television and mass media ads sets a child straight regarding the protocol of gender in the United States. By age two or three, children begin to sort out how they fit in, and, by puberty, gender identity is usually clearly fixed. As adults, we recognize that there is a spectrum of identities along the continuum and learn to adjust. We don't all park ourselves at the far ends of the gender teeter-totter—macho dude or girly girl. Despite efforts by parents to broaden the choices, the larger culture's assumptions about gender are very alluring for children. They learn through interactions with media and other children that it's best to jump into one of the two boxes that we explored in chapter one.

Although our culture assumes that natal men express their gender as male and natal women as female, in practice a wide variety of choices are exhibited here as well. In essence we "perform" or "act out" our gender role for others through our **gender expression**. The choices that we make might be conscious or unconscious. For example, I teach at an urban community college. My students are predominantly Latina/o, so the standard wardrobe for females is form-fitting jeans and blouses, often low-cut enough to show cleavage, and false fingernails and large earrings are the norm. Males, on the other hand, wear baggy, very low-slung pants and oversized t-shirts, and precise, pencil-thin beard lines are quite common. If I ask why they choose to deck themselves out in this manner, quite a few of them don't consider their clothing or grooming as consciously chosen. Others say that they are comfortable or that they like that look.

Most of us are quite aware of our choice of costume—no man, for example, accidentally wears a skirt to work—but, unless we study details of vocal inflection, most of us pay no attention to how our use of cadence and melody mirrors what our culture has taught us about how men and women speak. The woman who avoids qualifiers such as "It seems" and tag questions such as "Do you agree?" is likely to be read as forceful and domineering, i.e. not acceptably feminine. Also, we simply gesture when we speak, not bothering to check if we hold our elbows in tight enough to model feminine behavior or out far enough to look masculine. To check this, as you interact with people on a given day, pay attention to gender expression by asking yourself, "Where along the continuum of male and female is this person presenting in voice, action, costume and bodily adornment?"

That exercise is an example of **gender attribution**, the way we read the gender expressions of others.[29] Unlike the exercise above, however, we don't pay attention to the process of perception and we normally don't think in terms of a continuum or spectrum of possible choices. We stay with the boy/girl paradigm. As a result, when we meet a new person, the first thing that we notice is gender. We observe body parts, dress, personal grooming and mannerisms then make a quick attribution, a snap judgment: "This is a guy" or "This is a girl." We make this judgment mindlessly, and if we can't sort out gender immediately we become disoriented and uncomfortable because we then have to pay attention and consciously splice together clues to build evidence that allows us to hazard a guess. Once we have made the attribution, the assumption that we make controls how we to relate to the person in subtle and even overt ways. I, for example, quite often will engage in male-bonding banter, mildly teasing a new acquaintance to test for a sense of humor, but only if I assume the person to be a man.

41

I don't remember ever doing this upon first meeting someone who I judged to be a woman.

Finally there is **sexual orientation**, and there is much more at play here than merely being straight or gay, especially when we consider that the degree of attraction we feel for others is based upon their gender expression as much as their natal sex, which is inferred until a relationship is already established. Beyond that, the terms *straight* and *gay* are not very precise because they assume a connection between a person's sense of attraction and her/his natal sex. Consider a transsexual, born with a penis and testicles, who has had surgery and now has a clitoris and vagina. Is her attraction to women now considered gay or straight? The problem with *gay* and *straight* is that they have the same conceptual limitation as *homosexual* and *heterosexual*— all these terms define the attraction in terms of the sex of the person feeling the attraction. *Androphilia* (attraction to males) and *gynophilia* (attraction to females) are more accurate terms in that they separate the attraction from the sex or gender of the person experiencing that attraction.[30] *Gay* and *straight*, however, are not only deeply ingrained in our thinking about gender and sex, they also have the benefit of being simple one-syllable words, so they are unlikely to leave common usage. It can be a challenge to use them accurately when speaking of trans people, however. Trans people use these terms with their affirmed gender as the reference point and expect others to use them in the same way. A female-to-male transsexual who is attracted to men is likely to be insulted if he is referred to as straight or heterosexual because he identifies as male and considers himself to be gay. One way to clarify this issue is to match your use of such terms to the person's preferred pronoun. If he prefers *he* and *him* and is attracted to men, he's gay.[31]

Although the binary separation in the table above can be a useful tool in sorting out the difference between gender and sex, it has the disadvantage of reinforcing the popular notion that men and women are diametric opposites. That notion assumes that each of us is male or female, nothing in between, and certainly not a blend of the two. A great deal of money has been made, especially in the past few decades, by reinforcing this sense of separateness. John Gray of *Mars and Venus* fame has built an entire industry that fortifies and exalts gender polarization.

Humor helps to anchor our assumptions about this polarization. To understand how, read through the following stock jokes:

- A woman marries a man expecting he will change, but he doesn't. A man marries a woman expecting that she won't change, but she does.
- What is the difference between men and government bonds? Bonds mature.
- What did God say after he created man? I can do better than this.
- Do you know how men define a 50/50 relationship? We cook/they eat; we clean/they dirty; we iron/they wrinkle.
- Did you hear they finally made a device that makes cars run 95% quieter? Yeah, it fits right over her mouth.
- If your dog is barking at the back door and your wife is yelling at the front door, who do you let in first? The dog of course: at least he'll shut up after you let him in.
- One golfer tells another, "Guess what! I got a set of golf clubs for my wife." The other replies, "Great trade!"
- Why is it difficult to find men who are sensitive, caring and good looking? They already have boyfriends.

These jokes are funny only within a paradigm that polarizes gender, defining men and women as not only separate from but also antagonistic or even abusive toward each other. I am not arguing that we should be humorless about gender and sexuality. My point is that we can benefit from distinguishing and acknowledging what our humor assumes. It is unrealistic, however, to expect ourselves to suddenly and magically live outside a paradigm that is so deeply ingrained in us by our culture. The challenge is to notice how that paradigm, the lens we use to examine gender, dictates what we are able to see. Sandra Bem, a feminist psychologist, says that we benefit if we can occasionally look *at* the lens instead of always naively looking *through* it. When we think about gender, our culture teaches us to polarize everyone into two sexes and to ignore evidence of two things: that there may be more than two sexes, and that the two culturally accepted sexes may be more alike than different.

Bem argues that the separation is based not on fact but on cultural assumptions and that reinforcement of those assumptions damages our sense of common humanness. Before Bem's work, tools for measuring masculinity and femininity assumed that a person might be either masculine or feminine to a varying degree but that nobody could be both. In contrast, Bem mapped masculinity and femininity as two distinct scales that are neither polar opposites nor mutually exclusive. She developed the Bem Sex Role Inventory in the late 1970s, which was designed so that a person might rank high or low on either or both of these scales.[32] Her results showed that people of both natal sexes score in a variety of ways on the inventory, and a person might score high in masculinity and also high in femininity. Bem's premise is that we would better understand each other if our thinking about gender could be more flexible and if cultural stereotypes of gender were not so predominant in our thinking.

Clarification of Terms

Upon first exposure to gender nonconformity, the confusion parents feel is often intensified by a barrage of terms that feel foreign and can be intimidating. The list below, though not exhaustive, provides a basic understanding of words and phrases that are often used in conversations about gender nonconformity and transgender treatment.

Affirmed Female/Male: A recently adopted phrase for male-to-female (MTF) or female-to-male (FTM) that is considered more trans-friendly. Use of this term avoids the use of *trans*, which suggests that a person is somehow "between" or "on the way to somewhere but not there yet."

Agonist/Antagonist: These are terms that you may hear endocrinologists use in connection to hormone blockers. After an *agonist* such as testosterone or estrogen attaches to a receptor in the body, it creates a specific action or response in the surrounding cells. In contrast, a hormone blocker is an *antagonist*. When it attaches to the receptor it creates no action, thus "blocking" the action (pubertal change) that the testosterone or estrogen would normally create.

Androgyny: Gender expression that is not clearly male or female or is a mix of the two.

Being Read: Not passing as male or female despite attempting to do so.

Butch: Traditionally used describe a lesbian whose gender identity and/or expression is masculine. Sometimes now used to describe any woman who presents as masculine. Also used as noun.

Cisgender: An adjective that identifies conventional gender identity and expression. A natal male who identifies as male and "looks" male is cisgender. He is clearly seen as male without having to concern himself about how he expresses gender. This term is often used to point out the "privilege of passing." I, for example, am comfortable with being assigned as male and don't have to consciously portray my maleness in order to be read as male by others. I also don't have to concern myself that I might be gawked at and snickered at in public—or worse, be abused or assaulted today and hear tomorrow in court that I provoked the attack.[33]

Conversion Therapy (also Reparative Therapy): Traditionally applied to therapeutic treatment intended to "cure" homosexuality, this term has also been used to refer to similar treatment for transsexuality and gender nonconformity, especially in children. Conversion therapy for homosexuality has been formally opposed by the APA since 1997[34] and also by a host of other professional organizations. This term has also been used to describe therapy designed to realign gender-nonconforming behavior in young children. The most prominent therapist who uses this approach is Kenneth Zucker of Toronto's Centre for Addiction and Mental Health.[35]

Cross-sex hormone therapy: use of testosterone to masculinize or estrogen to feminize the body.

Cross Dresser: Traditionally, a man who dresses in women's clothing. Recently, the term has been used more broadly by some people to describe anyone who wears cross-gender clothing. The term does not designate anything about sexual orientation.

Drag King/Drag Queen: Performance roles in which the performer cross-dresses in a flamboyant, stereotypical manner. Traditionally, drag queens are natal males, usually homosexuals and drag kings are natal females, usually lesbians.

DSM: The *Diagnostic and Statistical Manual of Mental Disorders* is the guide used by psychotherapists in the United States. The fourth edition is currently being revised. Gender Identity Disorder first appeared in the *DMS-III*, published in 1980.

Femme: A lesbian whose gender expression is feminine and who is attracted to a butch lesbian.[36]

FTM: Female to male transsexual.

Gender attribution: The process, usually subconscious, that we use to decide whether a person is male or female.

Gender Binary: The assumption that there are two separate genders and that every person identifies as male or female.

Gender Continuum: In contrast to gender binary, the belief that there are endless ways to express and experience gender. People may identify as male, female or something between.

Gender Confirmation Surgery: A more affirming term for gender reassignment surgery or, worse, sex reassignment surgery.

Gender Dysphoria: Discomfort with one's natal sex and with the gender roles that society assigns to that sex. This term is often used as a synonym for GID and is likely to replace Gender Identity Disorder in the DSM V.[37]

Gender Expression: The ways in which we "perform" gender. We act out our gender through voice, apparel, mannerisms and a variety of other tools of self-expression.

Gender Fluid: sometimes used as an equivalent to gender queer, but more often describes a person whose gender identity and/or expression differs depending upon mood or situation.

Gender Identification: The self-identity that a person has in relation to masculinity and femininity. Using our understanding of our culture's definition of acceptable gender roles, we determine where we fit in. In essence we figure out how male or female we are.

Gender Queer/Queer: Purposely presenting gender expression that does not fit clearly into one of the polar extremes of male or female. This term has gained popularity with people, mostly under thirty, who are openly expressing their rejection of the assumed binaries of gender and sexual orientation. For those who remember the use of queer as a slur, the term has ugly reverberations, but today, it is being reclaimed much as *black* was reclaimed during the civil rights movement. Other terms that might be used: *bigender, pangender, agender, other-gendered.*

Gender Roles: The behaviors assumed by a culture to define masculinity and femininity. Our culture's construction of gender defines for each of us which behaviors are male and which female.

Gender-nonconforming: Not fitting within gender stereotypes. This is perhaps the most general term used to describe those who do not fit into the assumed binary view of gender.

Gender-variant: gender-nonconforming. Although the difference between the two may seem insignificant, *variant* suggests deviance and abnormality.

Genderism: Akin to racism or sexism. Assuming that every person's gender identity and expression must match culturally defined stereotypes and that there is something clearly wrong or disturbing about those who violate such stereotypes.

GID/GIDC: Gender Identity Disorder/Gender Identity Disorder in Children. These are the two possible official diagnoses that therapists can assign to a client who is seeing them regarding problems with gender. They are described in detail in the *Diagnostic and Statistical Manual of Mental Disorders* (DSM) of the American Psychological Association.

HRT (hormone replacement therapy): The prescription and use of estrogen by post menopausal women. Although inaccurate, this phrase is sometimes used in reference to cross-sex hormone therapy. See the discussion of hormone therapy later in this chapter.

Hormone Blockers: Compounds that halt puberty by blocking the receptors for testosterone or estrogen. There is a full explanation later in this chapter.

Intersex: A condition in which a person's natal sex is uncertain because of any number of medical conditions or variations in fetal development. This might be diagnosed at birth because of genital variation, but can also go undetected throughout a person's life. Previously referred to as *hermaphroditism*, a term that is offensive to intersex people and should be avoided.

MTF: Male to female transsexual.

Non-op: An adjective that describes transsexual who does not intend to have gender confirmation surgery. This could apply to a trans man who has chest reconstruction but not genital surgery.

Out/Coming Out: Just as with gays and lesbians, transsexuals usually determine that to live life with integrity, they must openly state their inner sense of who they are to others.

Packing: Wearing some sort of padding such as a rolled up sock or prosthesis to give the appearance of having a penis and testicles.

Passing: Being accepted by others as unquestionably male or female. Unlike those who pass without a conscious decision or effort to do so, gender-nonconforming people must decide if they want to pass and, if they do, how to represent themselves convincingly. See cisgender and gender queer.

Post-op: An adjective that describes a transsexual who has had gender confirmation surgery.

Pronoun Preference: She/he, his-him/her: these often become problematic when used around gender-nonconforming people. Some people prefer gender-neutral substitutes. The most widely used being *zie* (pronounced ZEE) and *hir* (pronounced HEER). When in doubt, it's best to simply ask.

Pre-op: An adjective that describes a transsexual who intends to have gender confirmation surgery.

Sex Affirmation Surgery: Gender confirmation surgery.

Sex Reassignment Surgery (SRS): The traditional phrase to describe a variety of surgeries that are used to align a transsexual's genitalia with her/his gender identification. This term is widely considered to be disrespectful of trans people.

Standards of Care (SOC): Guidelines for treatment of people with gender dysphoria. See the discussion immediately following this list of terms.

Stealth: Passing effectively in one's assumed gender and purposely not calling attention to the fact. A trans person who is *stealth* blends in with the conventionally gendered culture and does not want to be known as part of the transgender community. Of course, it is possible for a person to operate in *stealth mode* in some settings but not others.

Trans: Used as an adjective in a global way. The term can be used singularly ("She's a trans woman," or "He is trans.") or more expansively ("The trans community"). *Trans* does not necessarily mean transsexual, so *the trans community* would include anyone who does not fit into the limits of binary gender assumptions.

Transgender: Used in a variety of ways, this term is often used to define a broad spectrum of identities. It is often used as an equivalent to gender-nonconforming but may have any number of other, more specific meanings, depending upon usage and context. A person who says, "I am transgender," might mean, "I am an FTM," or, "I am gender queer," or "I am gender fluid," or . . .

Transition: The process of progressing from female to male or vice versa through gender expression, hormone therapy, and/or surgery. Also used in a more limited way to describe the moment that a person "switches" gender.

Trans Man: A natal female who identifies as male.

Transsexual: A person whose gender identity contradicts her/his natal sex. Traditionally, this term has referred only to people who have had or intend to have gender confirmation surgery, but it's meaning varies greatly depending upon who is using the term and in what context. Sometimes this term is used very broadly as a synonym for gender-nonconforming.

Transvestite: Cross dresser. This term seems to be falling out of use.

Trans Woman: A natal male who identifies as female.

Now that we have defined these terms, let's examine the history that they grew out of. What follows will track the treatment of transsexuality and GID and provide a background for the paradigm that our culture uses to understand transgenderism.

A Brief History of the Treatment of Transsexualism in the United States

The tradition of treatment for transsexualism in the United States dates back to the 1950s, when Harry Benjamin, a New York-based endocrinologist, treated hundreds of adult transsexuals. Benjamin used his long-standing relationship with Magnus Hirschfeld, a German psychiatrist who one of the most prominent early thinkers in sexology and who coined the terms *transvestite* and *transsexual*, to help patients find doctors in Germany who would perform surgery. Benjamin's protocol, referred to commonly as the Benjamin Standards of Care, provided the basis for treatment for transsexualism in the United States. Current management of the Standards of Care is overseen by WPATH (the World Professional Association for Transgender Health, Inc.), which has recently updated the Standards of Care to allow the psychotherapist far more latitude to adapt treatment so that if fits the need of each client.

John Money is another prominent figure in the treatment of transsexualism. Far more flamboyant, press-savvy and controversial than Benjamin, Money founded the Gender Identity Clinic at Johns Hopkins University in 1966 and was highly influential. With his insistence, the Clinic became the first to offer genital surgery for transsexuals in the United States. He managed to gain favorable press, and additional clinics opened at other universities, notably Stanford and the University of Minnesota. Money may have been the first sexologist to differentiate gender identity from sexual orientation,[38] and the conclusions that he drew from his research determined the treatment of adult transsexuals as well as intersex children for decades. He held the opinion that children begin life gender-neutral and that they adapt without issue to the gender in which they are raised. He considered the birth of an intersex child to be a psychological emergency for the parents and the child, advising that the medical team choose a sex for the child immediately, intervene surgically as early as possible in an effort to "normalize" the child's genitals, coach the parents to raise the child to conform to stereotypes of the assigned gender, and instruct the parents never to reveal the intersex condition to the child. Later in his career, Money acknowledged that the issue of gender was far more complex than he had believed early in his career.[39] Despite growing opposition, his approach to treatment of intersex children is still widely practiced in the United States.[40]

During the heyday of Money's approach, psychiatrists and medical doctors insisted that transsexual patients maintain a heterosexual orientation after surgery, meaning that the patient, always a trans woman (MTF) during this period, had to commit to sexual interaction only with men in order to receive surgery. Patients were quick to catch on and received coaching from previously successful candidates to assure that they would qualify for surgery.

Paul McHugh took over the psychiatry department at John Hopkins in 1975 and led a conservative backlash in the late 1970s, which closed down the university clinics, and the availability of safe surgery became far more scarce once again in the United States. Since then, surgery has been offered only by private clinics. Transsexuals gain entry to those clinics by being diagnosed with GID, and psychotherapists vary greatly in their opinion of GID as a diagnosis for adults as well as for children. Some therapists see GID as a serviceable diagnosis that can be used to help adult patients receive medical and social services. Others feel strongly that gender nonconformity, even in its most overt forms, is not pathological, does not qualify as a disorder and should be eliminated from the *DSM*. Yet others argue that GID should be eliminated because of its international impact. They argue that retaining it as a disorder in the U.S. encourages discrimination in cultures that stigmatize mental illness, which undermines efforts in those cultures to provide support and services for trans people.[41]

As for children who exhibit gender nonconformity, a few therapists agree with Kenneth Zucker that peer ostracism creates so much anxiety for a child that therapy to alter the child's behavior is warranted; furthermore, they believe that adult transsexualism should be avoided if possible and that behavior modification therapy for children is justified even though its impact on the eventual outcome is as yet unproven. Others feel that therapy should focus on helping the child to explore feelings and anxieties around gender, in essence working with the child without predetermined outcomes in mind. Parents and therapists who follow this regimen put their efforts into keeping communication open to discover together with their child the best path to follow. Rather than trying to reform their child's behavior, these parents work actively to change societal assumptions and to reform the culture that surrounds their child. Efforts include initiatives to promote acceptance of difference, to create supportive environments, and to include gender identity and expression in anti-bullying initiatives.

The Current State of Transsexuality in the United States

Although transsexuality has traditionally been considered a psychological disorder, this assumption is being challenged by reformers who argue that transsexuality and all forms of gender nonconformity are merely natural variations. Even though the reformist view is gaining traction, and there are many trans people who are quite well adjusted and may not consider themselves disordered in any way, the decision to access hormone therapy and surgery is a significant undertaking and can be done only through the intervention of a qualified psychotherapist.

Treatment begins with the psychotherapist documenting that the patient qualifies for treatment under the Standards of Care, which were updated in 2011, and the update recognizes multiple possible outcomes and provides far more flexibility than previous versions have allowed. For adults, treatment might or might not include hormone therapy and/or surgery. Prior to genital surgery, the patient has lived full-time in gender s/he identifies with. This is commonly referred to as the "real-life experience,"[42] This restriction does not hold for other surgeries. For example, it is not unusual for a female-to-male transsexual to have chest reconstruction surgery before undertaking the real-life experience. The SOC allow a therapist considerable leeway to determine the best treatment for each individual.[43]

Not all gender-nonconforming adults desire to pursue full transition. Some are content to live part-time in each gender. It is not unusual for a male cross dresser to wear women's clothing only in private, and there are cases of people living openly in a cross-gender role with no hormone replacement or surgery. One of the most famous cases was that of jazz musician, Billy Tipton, who lived as a man but was discovered to have a woman's body by a mortician. Some people also consciously refuse to "pass," and either purposely present themselves androgynously or purposely switch between male and female presentation. I have heard therapists and care providers claim that this choice is restricted to college students who eventually realize that they must choose a more conventional gender expression once they leave the accepting campus environment and enter the work force, but increasingly this is not the case. One example is Judith/Jack Halberstam who teaches at the University of Southern California, presenting her/himself as Judith at times and or Jack at others.[44]

Although the real-life experience may seem to be the least profound aspect of transition, it has a permanence that is unique for a trans person. As mentioned elsewhere, there is less room to maneuver for the natal male than the natal female. A trans man might play with butch presentation extensively without anyone taking much notice. He can wear his hair very short yet be seen merely as pixie-ish, and he is unlikely to attract attention if he wears pants and a shirt from the men's department.[45] He can revert back to a more feminine expression the next day without anyone making a comment. But a trans woman faces a different challenge because the markers of femininity are off-limits for a man. Consider what those markers are: makeup, heels, skirts, necklaces, bracelets, earrings. If she ventures out of the house wearing any of these markers, people not only take notice but remember.

For children, the therapeutic process is necessarily more prolonged since genital surgery before the age of eighteen is not an option in almost all countries. Research has shown that the majority of adolescents who identify as transsexual will continue to be transsexual as adults. For younger children, however, the picture is not so clear, and the likelihood of a specific outcome is difficult to predict. A few researchers suggested general patterns, however. There is evidence, for example, that younger children who meet the "complete diagnostic criteria for GID according to the *DSM-IV*" are likely to have a transsexual outcome as adults.[46] Traditionally, it has been argued that three-quarters of boys who are diagnosed with GIDC will be homosexual as adults, not transsexual. This conclusion, based originally on Richard Green's fifteen-year longitudinal study that followed 44 boys who exhibited feminine behaviors,[47] has been challenged, and recent research on over 3000 subjects suggests that half the children who are treated for GIDC will end up homosexual or bisexual,[48] a significantly lower prevalence than assumed by Green, but still one hundred times the prevalence of homosexuality in the general population. Research to date does not provide a clear answer as to whether gender nonconformity is likely to persist into adulthood, but there is limited evidence that just over one quarter of children (27%) persist and that the persistence rate is 50% for FTM-identified children and 20% for MTF-identified children.[49] These ratios are based on one small sample and more research is needed to determine their accuracy.

Two Paths of Treatment for Young Children

Treatment for children takes one of two paths, each based on a differing set of assumptions. The traditional path has been behavioral modification, which attempts to "realign" the child's behavior so that it matches stereotypical behaviors of the gender that matches the child's natal sex. In the case of a boy, for example, the parents and therapist work as a team to discourage him from wearing dresses and playing with dolls and encourage him to display stereotypical male behaviors such as ball playing and rough-and-tumble play. As explained by the most prominent practitioner of this method, Kenneth Zucker of the Centre for Addiction and Mental Health in Toronto, Ontario, the rationale behind this approach is that suppressing cross-gender behavior treatment assures that the child will face less peer ostracism and might be less likely to have a transsexual outcome as an adult.[50] There is, however, no clear evidence as to the effect such intervention has on the child's eventual identification as an adult. The majority of therapists and medical professionals that I have spoken with disagree vehemently with Zucker's approach, considering the practice akin to conversion or reparative therapy for homosexuality and arguing that it reduces parents to the role of gender cops.[51]

The alternative approach is for the parents to work with a therapist to determine whether and how to limit the child's gender expression.

The first step is to do nothing—essentially waiting to see what develops. If the child is happy with expressing gender-atypical behavior at home but not in public, no action need be taken. But if the child exhibits clear discomfort at such an arrangement and insists on more open expression, the parents and therapist need to work with the child to determine how best to proceed. There are myriad issues to balance in this equation:

- the child's self assuredness
- the child's level of anxiety and sensitivity to peer responses
- the ability of the parents to agree about how to approach the issues involved
- the potential to control or alter peer ostracism through school intervention
- the family's finances
- the impact on siblings
- the degree of acceptance of the larger family
- the attitudes and flexibility of the school and community climate

The decisions and considerations are many and complicated. If the child cannot bear to be boxed in to gender-conforming expression, the parents need to determine when it might be appropriate to help the child "transition" to the cross-gender expression. Among the parents that I have spoken to, this has happened as early as age five.[52]

After transition, the family sits in a different kind of limbo, paying close attention to how the child identifies with the approach of puberty and looking for signs of what psychologists refer to as *desistence* or *persistence*. If the child desists, no longer identifying as the other sex, it is possible to transition back to the gender that matches natal sex; if the child persists, it is possible to forestall puberty by blocking adolescent hormones to provide additional time. The point is to allow time for careful consideration of the complexities involved. Not all children with cross-gender identification persist to become adult transsexuals, and for those who do not, current evidence shows that the developmental delay provided by hormone blockers is completely reversible. The child who desists can simply go off the blockers and go through puberty consistent with natal sex. For the child who persists, however, the blockers avoid the onset of bodily changes that would involve considerable surgical intervention, especially for natal boys, and significant financial burden because in the United States insurance coverage for such surgery is rare.

Which therapeutic path is better? That question plagues parents. Since there are no clear indications of long-term results, there is no absolute answer. The questions multiply: Does early intervention to suppress cross-gender expression "damage" the child's sense of self? Does it lessen the potential for adult transsexualism? If yes, is it ethical to intervene in order to avoid adult transsexualism? If you accept cross-gender behavior and allow your child to transition, are you increasing the chances that your child will become a transsexual as an adult? At what age do you trust your child's judgment regarding profound decisions? The challenge is to sort out which answers will result in the child growing into a happy adult with intact self-esteem. Since research yields no clear answers to any of these questions, there is no way of assuring that outcome, and parents simply have to make the most insightful decisions they can and then deal with the outcome.[53]

Prevalence of Transsexualism and Gender Nonconformity

So, how prevalent are transsexualism and gender nonconformity in adults and children? That has been an open question for decades. The prevalence of adult MTF transsexualism is estimated to be 1:30,000 by the *DSM-IV*, the prevalence most often cited in the press, but the number is based on very old research. Several people have offered information that the condition is far less rare than that, and the APA has issued an update that places adult MTF prevalence at 1:11,900 and adult FTM prevalence at 1:30,400.[54] Sam Winter, a prominent researcher of transsexualism in Asia, provides evidence that MTF prevalence in college-age Thai students exceeds 1:150.[55] Lynne Conway, a professor emerita at the University of Michigan, is a well-known trans woman and trans advocate. On her website, she jokes that psychologists don't seem to be able to count and offers compelling evidence that the *DSM-IV* figure is drastically low. She argues that since there are 32,000 post-op MTFs in the United States and the nation has roughly 80 million men aged 18-60 (the age range that would match post-op MTFs), we have a prevalence of 1:2500. Keeping in mind that this represents only post-operative transsexuals, which are a fraction of MTFs, Conway comes up with a prevalence of

1:500, which would make adult MTF transsexualism sixty times more prevalent than the *DSM*-suggests.[56] Other research, expanding on Conway's approach, puts the prevalence of MTFs at 1:750 and the prevalence of FTMs at 1:1400.[57] Conway has also collaborated recently with a Dutch team of researchers who have calculated the prevalence of MTF to range from 1:2,000-1:1,000 and the prevalence of FTMs range from 1:4,000-1:2,000.[58] The question remains as to why the prevalence of FTMs is so much lower than that of MTFs, although it has often been argued in trans circles that trans men pass far more easily than trans women and that it is likely that many FTMs live in stealth mode never to be detected. Of course, there is no means of testing that theory. Also, many people have pointed out that since gender roles are more restrictive at all ages for males than for females, the higher apparent incidence of MTFs is hardly surprising.

Prevalence for children (GIDC) is of particular concern because it seems to be increasing. The psychologists that I have spoken to are of the opinion that prevalence has not risen but that our attention to it has. The *DSM-IV* does not provide numbers, but Kenneth Zucker and Susan Bradley of the Toronto clinic have noticed a significant increase in referrals, which they attribute to the center's heightened visibility and to more thorough media coverage of gender nonconformity.[59] Zucker and Bradley have estimated the prevalence of GIDC to be between two and five percent of the general population.[60] The United States Census Bureau recorded the population of children between ages five and eighteen as 61.6 million in 2007, which would mean that up to three million children will exhibit some form of GIDC. If as many as three million children are significantly gender-nonconforming, it is seems almost certain that every school system in the nation has gender-nonconforming students, and we are hard-pressed to claim that it is rare or even uncommon.

Medical Interventions

Some of the most disquieting questions that parents face are about their child's health. What are the medical decisions and procedures that might be involved, and what are the risks of those procedures? A variety of issues needs to be considered, including psychotherapy, hormone therapy, and surgery. In addition, parents must consider the extent to which medical insurance will cover each of these.

We have already covered some of the issues regarding psychotherapy, but the first step in the process is to find a social worker, psychologist or psychiatrist with expertise in dealing with gender identity. This is not always easy because very few graduate programs in the U.S. offer training about the needs of homosexuals and even fewer offer their students any exposure to gender nonconformity or transsexuality. It is not mandatory, however, to find a therapist who is trained in matters of gender immediately. Some parents that I have spoken to worked successfully with a therapist who had no specialized training yet related well to their child and was willing to learn with the family. One family finally found a gender-trained specialist but went back to their original "untrained" psychologist because they sensed that the specialist was steering the child toward an outcome that promoted the therapist's agenda.

Of course, the choice of therapist depends upon the details of each situation. One divorced mom, whose eight-year-old son had spoken about suicide, knew that she needed to affirm his gender nonconformity rather than challenge it. Facing a custody battle with her ex-husband, who argued that she was forcing their son into a perverse charade, she needed to find a qualified psychologist to testify in court. In such a case, it is imperative to find someone with credentials that demonstrate expertise. To complicate the issue further, the mother would weaken her case if *she* were to choose the therapist. Instead, she needed to rely upon someone recommended by her son's pediatrician or another professional.[61] In this situation, she could not allow it to seem as if she has picked a sympathetic therapist who ascribed to her agenda.[62]

This case demonstrates some of the complexities that a parent might need to consider. Although the mom wants a therapist who will provide the support and guidance that her son needs, she must weigh her son's immediate psychological needs against long-term legal implications because a therapist who the judge assumes to have been hand-picked by the mother might jeopardize the mother's right to custody.[63]

Medical insurance poses an additional obstacle, and it is worthwhile for a family to explore options up front. Most insurance companies in the U.S. do not cover any medical expenses related to gender nonconformity or transsexuality, arguing that all such treatments reflect lifestyle choice and are "elective." Despite that, a diagnosis that cites hormonal abnormality or imbalance rather than gender dysphoria might result in hormone blockers or hormone therapy being covered. It is even possible that surgery might be covered, at least partially. For example, our child managed to have nose feminization partially covered when she had a deviated septum repaired. The surgeon was dual certified in plastic surgery and otolaryngology, so out-of-pocket expenses were considerably less than we would have paid otherwise. Help might also be available through an employer. For example, corporate policy for a few companies dictates that all medical expenses related to transsexuality are covered by insurance, including all surgery.[64]

Aside from legal and insurance concerns, parents need to know what medical issues are involved. How do hormone blockers work? What are the risks of taking hormones? Who are the best surgeons? What are the surgical procedures? How successful is the outcome of surgery and what are the risks involved? Since insurance won't cover it all, how much is this going to cost? What about fertility?

Medical options for young children are fully discussed in *The Transgender Child* by Stephanie Brill and Rachel Pepper. There is no need to repeat all the details here, but the issues to consider are as follows:

- Before accepting medical advice, investigate how knowledgeable the doctor is and how well researched the offered opinion is.
- Prepare yourself and your child for issues that may arise in a medical emergency.
- Assure that your child has a therapist on board well before the onset of puberty so a diagnosis is available to allow hormone blockers as an option.
- Educate yourself about hormone blockers and hormone therapy.
- Know the WPATH Standards of Care.

Hormone Therapy

When a persisting, gender-nonconforming child approaches puberty, cross-sex hormone therapy needs to be considered. Decisions regarding this need to be made with as full an understanding of

research as possible, and parents, child and their team of professionals should work together to determine how to proceed. A child who
is distraught with bodily changes and who persists in the desire for
cross-gender behavior is likely to benefit from additional time to sort
out what is going on. A pediatric endocrinologist can prescribe medications to delay the onset of puberty to buy that additional time. The
most prominent proponent of this approach in the United States is
Dr. Norman Spack, an endocrinologist with Children's Hospital in
Boston. Spack explains that the delay of puberty allows adequate time
to carefully consider how to proceed. Delaying puberty also foregoes
the trauma of going through puberty in the "wrong sex" then having
to undergo multiple surgeries to reverse the process.

The preferred time to intervene with blockers is at what pedia-
tricians call Tanner scale 2. Most parents have not heard of the Tanner scale (or stage) prior to discussions with their child's pediatrician,
but it is relatively simple. Developed by James M. Tanner, an English
pediatrician to measure sexual development during puberty, the scale
runs from 1, no adolescent development, to 5, adult development. If
hormone blocking is to be effective, it needs to happen relatively early
in the process, thus Tanner scale 2, and certainly not later than 3.

Girls at Tanner scale 2 exhibit enlarged areolas with breast buds,
an enlarged clitoris with labia pigmentation, sparse growth of slightly
pigmented hair along the labia. They gain height at 2 3/4 to 3 1/4
inches per year. At Tanner scale 3 their breasts elevate beyond areola
borders, their public hair darkens and curls and they continue the
same growth rate.

Boys at Tanner scale 2 show a thinning and reddening of the
scrotum, sparse growth of slightly pigmented hair at the base of penis,
decrease in body fat, growth of the testicles to between 1 and 1 1/4
inches in breadth. They gain height at the rate of 2 to 2 1/3 inches per
year. At Tanner scale 3, the pubic hair is courser and curly; testicle
breadth reaches 1 1/2 inches, the penis begins to lengthen and body
height continues to increase at a rate of about 3 inches per year.

So how do blockers actually work? The simplest explanation is
that testosterone or estrogen fits into receptors throughout the body,
much like a key fits into the lock of a door. Let's take a girl for example. She has receptors for estradiol, the form of estrogen produced by
the ovaries, in her brain, breasts, heart, blood vessels, uterus, vagina,
bladder, liver, bones, skin, and gastrointestinal tract. . Upon reaching

puberty, her ovaries go into overdrive and flood the bloodstream with estradiol, which travels through her system looking to "key in" to the receptors. When blockers are administered, they attach to the receptors so that the door is "closed" when the estrogen flows by.

A different approach for natal boys is to use GnRH (gonadotropin-releasing hormone) agonists, which function differently. Rather than blocking the receptors, they act on the pituitary gland. At first, they overstimulate it but then desensitize it to GNRH so that after several weeks, production of testosterone is greatly reduced, which is exactly what is being sought. Simply put, a prescription of Tamoxifen or one of the GnRH agonists shuts down puberty.

Spack, who has treated over 200 adolescents, has come under attack by conservatives who argue that children cannot possibly understand the complexities of gender and that helping them to alter their gender is unethical. Beyond this, the critics insist that transsexualism and gender nonconformity are psychological disorders treatable only through psychotherapy and that Spack is "collaborating with" the disorder rather than curing it, thus making the patient's life worse.[65]

Others see the choice to block hormones as controversial because it interrupts the natural process of maturation. Dr. Polly Carmichael of the Portman Clinic in London explains:

> There are debates to be had around the impact of giving hormone blockers at an early stage. One of the debates is, indeed, [do] one's own sex hormones have an impact on identity development in adolescence? So if one intervenes, is that affecting the final outcome? I think that's just one part of the debate, but [it is] important to debate.
>
> What we're doing now is new, so it's appropriate to be exploring and discussing. And it's a plausible question—is one of the effects a change in final outcome?[66]

Since current research provides no absolute answers, parents are forced to proceed on the faith of their ability to gather information and evaluate its viability, maintain open communication with their child and work effectively with the medical/psychological team.

As if those concerns were not enough, there is another potential stumbling block: an adolescent on hormone blockers may benefit by buying additional time to contemplate the next move, but s/he is also not growing along with peers. Other boys will be shooting up inches a year, gaining muscle mass, shaving and speaking with new-found baritone voices of authority. Girls will continue to menstruate, develop full breasts, rounded hips and a defined waist. Conversations regarding these developments and the notice everyone takes of them are rampant, so the teen who still appears to be stuck at age twelve can feel left behind and can become a target for teasing, ostracism and bullying. The child is likely to require counseling and will certainly need parental support while all this is going on.

Perhaps the most difficult, and certainly most controversial, concern is fertility. A child who goes on blockers, persists, and then takes cross-sex hormones will almost certainly be sterile, and at the age of sixteen, it is impossible to sort out how much the loss of fertility might matter later in life. For most transgender adolescents, the agony of going through puberty the wrong direction as dictated by the natal hormones far outweighs the loss of fertility. That is not, to say, however, that the decision is easy for the child or the parents, and, as with many of the decisions that these families must make, there is no turning back. One study that surveyed 121 adults found that the vast majority of them felt that freezing sperm should be explored and a smaller majority of them would have chosen to bank sperm if there had been a means of doing so.[67] Also, a significant portion did not want to have their own children because of the chance that their transsexualism was hereditary.[68]

Spack essentially follows the Dutch protocol, which allows for blocking hormones early in adolescence, and he deals with the issue of fertility openly with parents and child, explaining that hormone blocking alone has no impact on fertility, but starting cross-sex hormone treatment virtually assures sterility. He points out, however, that the blocking certainly helps in that it is "a lot different to be talking to a 14-, 15-, 16-year-old about the implications of this than a 10- to 12-year-old."[69]

For Adults only: Surgical Procedures and Choices

One prominent secondary effect of testosterone is that it alters facial structure a great deal, and, although some of these changes can be de-emphasized with cosmetics, none of them can be altered without surgery. As a result, there is a host of surgical procedures that some MTFs feel they must undergo in order to pass as female effectively. The male forehead is flatter, the brow more pronounced, the hairline higher, the jaw line more prominent and the chin square rather than pointed. Below is a list of surgeries that an MTF might consider, including descriptions where needed and possible side effects.[70]

Blepharoplasty (Eyelid tuck): Restructuring of the eyelids. Most men have more fat deposits around the eyes than women, in the both upper lids (which cause wrinkles) and lower lids (which cause bags under the eyes to be more prominent). Side effects: possible scarring, but seldom prominent.

Breast augmentation: Many MTFs are concerned about breast size since it is such a clear cultural marker of femininity. Side effects: possible silicone leakage or relocation of the implant.

Facial bone reduction: This involves the brow and the chin. Side effects: numbness, which usually subsides within several months.

Genitoplasty: Gender affirmation surgery, either FTM or MTF.

Labiaplasty: Creation of inner labia from the scrotum. Sometimes completed as a secondary surgery following vaginoplasty, usually under local anesthetic. Risks are minimal.

Liposuction of the waist: To help create the traditionally-defined hour-glass contour. Side effects (all rare): lung blood clot, infection, abdominal perforation.

Orchiectomy, also Orchidectomy: Removal of the testes. This is usually done through an abdominal incision on each side of the penis, which leaves the scrotum intact for use in vaginoplasty. Certain side effect: sterility. Possible side effects: decreased libido (loss of interest in sex), erectile dysfunction, hot flashes, weight gain, loss of muscle mass, osteoporosis, and gynomastia (breast enlargement). Of course, most MTFs are hoping for this last development.

Perioral feminization (Lip lift/Lip augmentation): The space between the nose and the upper lip is larger in men, and a woman's upper lip reveals more of her teeth. The incision is made directly below the nose. The lips can be enhanced with synthetic inserts or fat deposits collected from elsewhere in the body. Possible side effect: uncertain results; additional surgery to address excessive bleeding or redistribution of fat to another part of the body.

Rhinoplasty: A nose job. Men's noses tend to be larger than women's. The nose also angles out more from the forehead. Finally the tip of a woman's nose is higher than a man's.

Rhytidectomy: A face lift.

Thyroid chondroplasty (Tracheal Shave): Reduction of the Adam's apple. Side effect: alteration of voice (Rare: happens only if too much cartilage is taken).

Vaginoplasty: Creation of a neo-vagina. The preferred method is "penile inversion." The outer skin of the penis becomes the vagina and the scrotum becomes the labia. The glans is scaled back and becomes the clitoris. Possible side effects: genital pain, scarring (hidden by pubic hair).

Despite the challenges that are faced with passing, given the advances in surgical procedures, an MTF who chooses to undergo genital surgery can expect to have an aesthetically pleasing, and fully functional vagina. In contrast, most FTMs can pass as younger males with relative ease, especially if they have started testosterone injections. Results are highly variable but can be rather dramatic with facial hair appearing within the first few months of therapy, and full effects are not seen for two years or more. Although these advantages are significant, FTMs have a different challenge: despite skilled efforts of surgeons and careful adherence to pre- and post-operative guidelines, an FTM cannot expect to have fully functioning genitalia after genital surgery.

Now for the surgical procedures that an FTM might consider:

Hysterectomy: Not necessary, but many FTMs prefer to have one.

Liposuction to reduce fat in hips, thighs, and buttocks: The purpose is to get rid of the female-pattern fat distribution. Possible side effects: uneven results, stretch marks.

Mastectomy/Chest reconstruction: There are several methods that might be used depending on the size of the breasts. After removal of the breast tissue, the surgeon constructs a masculine contour. Possible side effects: prominent scarring, numbness, possible loss of sensation in the nipples—or even loss of nipples (rare). Does not eliminate the potential for breast cancer. It is becoming more common for teens as young as sixteen to have this procedure performed.

Metoidioplasty (Clitoral release): After the clitoris has enlarged from testosterone, ligaments that hold it in place are severed, creating a small phallus (usually four or five centimeters long). There are generally no risks or side effects unless the urethra is lengthened to allow urination while standing. If this option is chosen, possible side effects include incontinence and multiple follow-up surgeries.

Oophorectomy: Removal of ovaries.

Phalloplasty: A high-risk, multiple-stage procedure that creates a penis with tissue from the abdomen (called a pedical flap or suitcase handle), or the flank or the forearm. Certain side effect: loss of sensation (the clitoris is not preserved); prosthesis needed for erection. Possible side effects: tissue atrophy; deterioration and narrowing of the lengthened urethra; urinary fistula—a complication with the urethra that creates incontinence; injury to tissue by erectile prosthetic. Patients often return for follow-up surgeries.

Scrotoplasty, also called Oscheoplasty): Construction of a scrotum from the labia major. This is often done at the same time as phalloplasty or metoidioplasty. Rather than attempting to complete the process in one operation, some surgeons prefer to insert small inflatable balloons used to gradually stretch the neo-scrotum to allow for insertion of silicone implants later (an out-patient procedure).

Vaginectomy: Required during phalloplasty or metoidioplasty if the patient chooses to have the urethra lengthened to allow for standing to urinate.

Bottom surgery for FTMs is often fraught with complications despite efforts of an experienced and skilled surgeon. Metoidioplasty is far safer and the outcome more predictable than phalloplasty. When complete it creates a small, but normal looking penis, and retains sensation in the clitoris. It does not result in a penis large enough for sexual intercourse. Patients who choose to undergo phalloplasty will face multiple surgeries and should expect complications.

Hair Removal

Hair, where it is or where it isn't, is a clear cultural sign of gender. FTMs are usually delighted with the resulting facial and body hair that sprouts from testosterone treatment, and a high percentage of them choose to sport some type of beard. MTFs, on the other hand, face the challenge of removing unwanted hair, sometimes thick masses of it. Although careful shaving can help hide a beard, especially if it is fine and light colored, most MTFs choose to have their beard removed either through electrolysis or laser treatment. Which to choose? The answer may be both. Our daughter has been going through electrolysis over a period of years and has opted to try laser then follow up with more electrolysis if needed.

Electrolysis, the only method of hair removal that the FDA recognizes as permanent, is a very meticulous procedure. The electrologist inserts a very fine probe into an individual hair follicle then subjects the follicle to a small electric shock. The main benefit is that once finished, it results in complete removal of the hair. The challenge, however, is to finish. The process is time consuming and expensive. With current rates of $80/hr or more, it often becomes the most expensive part of transition. Not all states regulate or license electrologists, so it is best to complete a careful background check that considers licensure, education, and affiliation with professional associations. It is also worthwhile to find out if the electrologist has experience treating transsexual clients and to request referrals to satisfied clients.

The process is not painless and requires multiple passes in the same area because each hair follicle must be treated separately, sometimes several times, and some hairs will be dormant at any given session. The pain can be addressed at least partially through the use of numbing lotions prior to treatment and oral analgesics. After treatment, skin is likely to be tender and may look inflamed, perhaps for several days. In addition, the process requires that hair be allowed to grow two or three days prior to the session.

In comparison, laser hair removal is generally less expensive per session and less time consuming because the laser beam treats an area of the face rather than individual follicles. However, skin may be tender after treatment, and exposure to the sun must be avoided before and after treatment. As with electrologists, oversight of laser technicians varies from state to state, and in some states treatment can only be provided under the supervision by a licensed physician. Results vary and are dependent upon skin and hair pigmentation with the best outcome being achieved on light skin with a dark beard. Laser is least effective on light or fine hair, especially on a dark complexion. Although laser treatment cannot claim *permanent* removal, some people find the result quite satisfactory.

In general, electrolysis costs more per session and per hair follicle treated than does laser treatment. When comparing prices, remember that a higher hourly rate charged by a particular practitioner does not necessarily mean that the entire process will cost more because an experienced or highly skilled practitioner may be more adept, covering more hairs during the session.

Beyond the beard, MTFs often look to have other areas addressed as well and those who pursue genital surgery need to consider treatment of the pubic area, especially the scrotum, which will be used to form the labia of the neo-vagina. This treatment should be undertaken in consultation with the surgeon. The surgeon often will scrape the scrotal skin and cauterize hair follicles during surgery, but some do not consider this adequate assurance of hair removal and may dictate that the patient undergo electrolysis prior to surgery.

There are risks involved with both methods. Improper laser treatment can result in permanent skin damage, especially on dark skin. Electrolysis may create scarring and can aggravate acne and psoriasis. Also, the technician for either should provide information about medications to avoid during treatment. For example, any medication that heightens light sensitivity must be avoided during laser treatment. Feel free to ask as many questions as you like. A responsible practitioner will be happy to address concerns.

CHAPTER 4

Momism, America's Contribution to Psychology: Who or What Is to Blame, Here?

"Pronouns"
by Irene Willis

When my son first told me, I didn't realize
I'd have to change the pronouns
shift their shapes to those I couldn't
fit my mouth around, or swallow.
He, him, his, rolled off my tongue like
marbles into the box of *she, her, hers.*
Where were the antecedents? *Whose?*
I whirled, searching our family of names.
Who was closest? Whom to blame?
But blame implies misdeed, and here was none.
My son, *mine.* I'd never had a daughter, never knew
I would give birth in what was now called "young old age."
Mother. Father. I grasped each noun like the pole
of a carousel. When I got off
the ground was still moving, and I was holding
his gold-embroidered past, and mine.[71]

T HE NARRATOR OF THE POEM above struggles with what
seems trivial on the surface. *Normal* parents never have to fret
over pronouns. They have the unrecognized luxury of using them

mindlessly, never needing to give *she/he her/him, her/his* any thought. *Normal* parents never have to consider how these pronouns help to keep us and our loved ones in their tidy boxes. For those of us with trans children, however, the simple act of referring to our children can become a moment of psychological torture. Something as simple as introducing our child to someone can create a moment of remorse: "Oh, I slipped up again! Did he—arrgh—she notice? How can this be so difficult? What is wrong with me, anyway?"

Wrong. What a powerful word! So much of what we experience around our child's abnormalness feels wrong. It's wrong to have to defend ourselves and our child, wrong that we are continually judged, wrong that our child is at risk, wrong that simple things are suddenly so complicated. And, just like the poem's narrator, when so much seems wrong, we look for someone to blame. It must be someone's fault, but who. In the United States, the answer is almost always Mom, and moms know it.

If you have never considered that your child's situation might be your fault, never experienced guilt about it, never worried if you somehow "caused" it, and have no interest in what *does* cause it, there is no need to read further. Skip this chapter. If, however, guilt or concern about causes is of interest, please read on—even if you are not a mom.

When we first learned that Cadence was transsexual, I wondered what it meant, but Karen wondered what she did wrong. Although rationally she was aware that she was not to blame, she seemed wired to worry and fret over the issue. Had she been too open in letting our boys (well, we had always assumed that they were both boys) explore any interest that seemed to amuse them as children. At age four, Cadence, then Jared, wanted a kitchen for Christmas. He had enjoyed baking bread with me since he was old enough to stand at the kneading board on a stool. We lived in a very conservative and provincial small town in Pennsylvania, and our lack of alignment with normalcy became apparent on a Saturday morning in December at a local breakfast nook. While taking our order, the chatty waitress asked, "So, what do you want for Christmas?" When the answer came back, "A kitchen," the waitress turned red and walked off to put our order in. Our child's simple utterance deflated all chattiness, and the waitress, though not cold, maintained her distance from that point on. Evidently she could think of nothing more to say to our deviant child.

Had Karen's hormone treatments brought on this deviance? Prior to Jared's birth, Karen had had two surgeries, had lost one ovary to endometriosis and had been on hormone injections for several years. Of course, *not* having the injections would have guaranteed that we had no children, but Karen still could not help wondering if the prenatal hormones had created a trans-friendly bath.[72]

Had her decision to nurse our kids until they weaned themselves created too strong a bond? Karen had nursed Jared for three years. Of course, there is a gigantic hole in the contention that she nursed too long, thus creating too strong a bond: Chad nursed even longer, yet he's quite happy in his male role and unquestionably heterosexual.

Karen's experience is not unusual. Here is a sampling of how other mothers have responded:

> As mother who carried her and gave birth to her, there was a lot of self-doubt. I ate all the right foods. I'm a vegetarian, but I thought, "Oh, my god, what did I do." I was an older mother. When Daphne was eight, she wanted to know why she felt like a boy and asked about what happened in the womb—what could go wrong. I did have one complication and wondered if that had something to do with it.

> I felt like I had failed him somehow, that I must have done something wrong—even though I couldn't think of what it might be.

> I was a single mom. Did I not give him what he needed?

> Was it because of something I did or because her dad was away so much?

> Did I cause her to feel this way? I dreamed of having a baby boy and was so sure it would be a boy that when the doctor said. "You have a beautiful daughter," I was in shock—just didn't believe him. Of course, when I saw her, I was fine with it, but I still feel guilt about how I felt.

> I went into therapy, and my therapist said, "I want to write down what you think you did." I said that I was too protective and said "I love you" too often to my son. He agreed!

Moms have been conditioned to respond to suffering with guilt: if your kid is suffering, it is somehow your fault. You may be in denial about it, but if you look deeply enough, you will find plenty of evidence that you were the cause of this pain. This assumption of pathology has become ingrained in our culture. As mentioned in chapter one, starting with Freud, therapists have found mothers to be the catalysts of any number of maladies in their children, and here in the U.S., there has been a long line of respected psychologists who have been willing to follow Freud's lead. Blaming Mom has become the American way. Guilt about "creating" difference in our children has become deeply entrenched, and the more different children seem in comparison to an assumed norm, the more guilty mom feels. Since transgenderism is right up there at the top of the wrongness list, mom gets treated to a proportional level of guilt. As a demonstration of this, during my interviews with mothers, it was very common to hear a mother say that she would have felt much better if her child could be "just gay."[73]

A Brief History of Momism

Social forces from the American Revolution and from the industrialization of the nation redefined motherhood as the creation of worthy citizens who would help build the nation, a goal that persists today. Effective child rearing had become a political obligation, and the burden of fulfilling that obligation fell primarily upon middle-class mothers. By the beginning of the twentieth century, faith in science had taken hold, and the nation looked to psychologists for guidance in child rearing, so much so that by the 1920s some felt that it would be best for children to be taken from their ignorant mothers, especially the poor ones, to be raised by professionals who knew what they were doing.[74]

The attack on mom gained traction at the advent of World War II with the 1942 publication of Philip Wylie's sensationalist best seller, *Generation of Vipers*, which he called a "sermon." In it, Wylie, a popular novelist and columnist, attacked essentially every aspect of American culture, describing the United States of the early 1940s as a feudal society and berating not only its moms but its religious leaders, school teachers, college professors, businessmen, politicians and soldiers. Although he devoted only one of his eighteen chapters to women, what he had to say in that chapter had staying power. Credited with coining the word *momism*, Wylie argued that women were now living too long and lacked productive activities to occupy them, so they had become manipulative, the result being that they used sentimentality to possess their sons' souls, thus totally controlling them.[75] Comparing their insidious power to Goebbels's ability to brainwash the German populace through the manipulation of mass media, Wylie claimed that moms had taken over male functions in our society and were controlling schools, churches, stores and mass production.[76]

This premise grew in prominence during the war, when some psychiatrists became alarmed that nearly two million young men were deemed to be unfit for military duty due to psychological disorders and that more than one million were either attempting to avoid the draft or were discharged for psychological reasons. The most prominent among these psychiatrists was Edward A. Strecker, who served in both World Wars and was chair of the Psychiatry Department at the University of Pennsylvania. Convinced that the nation was endangered by widespread psychological weakness, Strecker published two post-war books to address this problem: *Their Mothers' Sons* in 1946 and *Their Mothers' Daughters* ten years later. The first of these gained immediate prominence when the *Saturday Evening Post* published a condensed version of the book that carried the headline: "A Distinguished Psychiatrist Gives the Facts about Widespread Parental Failing." Despite the headline, Strecker was not particularly interested in facts from research data, but he was concerned about the state of the nation, and he separated *mothers* who raised mature, assertive citizens who furthered democracy from *moms* who raised immature, unthinking children who undermined national stability. His penchant for linking the domestic concerns of child rearing to global politics dovetailed with the post-war Red Scare, and he presented *moms*, who produced homosexuals and lesbians, as a threat to national security. Their insidious tactics seeped into our hapless society to the extent that even institutions such as labor unions, the bastions of the communist threat, functioned as moms. For Strecker, Hitler himself, with his hysterical ranting, had had the makings of a "super-mom."[77] If we accept

Strecker's assertions, American moms had become synonymous with the two most hideous threats to the wholesome American way.

Strecker was at the height of his influence in 1952 when transsexualism gained prominence with sensationalist headlines that covered Christine Jorgenson's sex change, and, as products of the era, professionals who treated transgender people in the 1950s and 1960s helped to perpetuate the sense of blame and shame. For example, although there is no indication that he considered transsexualism to be shameful, Harry Benjamin, who published *The Transsexual Phenomenon* in 1966, believed that his patients were "trapped in the wrong body," and that this wrongness needed to be cured or normalized. Since normalization was the goal, patients needed to fit the mold: after genital surgery they were to live "normal" lives, blending into society as heterosexual women.[78] Simply put, they were to disappear once they had been normalized, living in stealth mode, thus no different than any other "normal" woman. Benjamin assumed that gender was dichotomous (male/female—no other options) and that post-op transsexuals must be exclusively heterosexual in order to demonstrate that they had been transformed into orthodox women.[79] John Money's work at Johns Hopkins perpetuated the same assumptions and the same results, and the host of physicians and psychologists at the university clinics who followed Money's lead, accepted his approach without question—fix the deviant patient then see to it that she goes into hiding.

Money's early theory, as put forth when he opened the Gender Identity Clinic at Johns Hopkins, focused on normalization for children as well as adults, and he argued that a child's gender identity was molded in the early years and could be controlled through behavior modification. In the case of an intersex child, the genitals were to be normalized through surgery and the parents were to reinforce stereotypical gender behaviors, never revealing the truth to the child. As mentioned in chapter two, this shame-based approach still enjoys widespread acceptance today.[80]

In the case of a child who appeared to be anatomically normal but who did not fit the behavioral mold, the parents were to blame, especially the mother. Aside from John Money, other influential twentieth-century therapists who wrote about the mother's responsibility for gender nonconformity were Richard Green, Robert Stoller, Leslie Lothstein, George Rekers, and Kenneth Zucker. Green and

Stoller both served on the faculty at UCLA, and Green had been Money's student. In the 1960s, Stoller, who was far the more openly damning of the mother's influence than Green, began publishing case studies about feminine boys in academic journals, each study concluding that mothers were responsible for the malady.

Stoller argued that the source of a gender-nonconforming boy's behavior goes back two generations and originates with the maternal grandmother, a cold and unloving woman, especially toward her daughter. As a result the daughter identifies with her father (the boy's grandfather) but loses him at a young age through death or desertion, leaving her to feel abandoned and betrayed. She then marries a distant, passive husband, who will not challenge her dominance. When she has a son, she is delighted and works to create blissful life for him that is devoid of conflict, keeping him attached to her and arresting his natural masculine development. Although Stoller blames the boy's father for lacking the adequate masculine competence to intervene and thwart the mother's pathological, smothering nature, it is the mother who is the driving force in the poor child's road to psychological ruin.[81] As with Green, masculine girls are nowhere nearly as troubling for Stoller as feminine boys, but he argues that such girls are created by too close a relationship with the father. For him, a feminine boy or a masculine girl is created by the same parental error: thwarting the child's need to live out the Oedipus complex.[82]

Green's position was more subdued, and he started his 1974 book, *Sexual Identity Conflict in Children and Adults*, with a review of biological and psychological theories that had attempted to explain the origin of gender nonconformity and warned that the process of creating gender identity was too complex to be adequately explained by any single approach.[83] He reiterated this point in his chapter titled, "Feminine Boys: How They Got That Way," stating that only people with no actual knowledge of transgenderism claim to know what causes it and the more knowledge he had gained the less sure he had become about what he knew. On the following pages, however, he lists ten possible causes, one being an absent father. Can you guess who was the focus of the other nine?[84]

Unlike previous researchers, Leslie Lothstein, who co-directed the Case Western Reserve Gender Identity Clinic, focused on FTMs. In his 1983 book *Female-to-Male Transsexualism*, he asked why psychologists had ignored FTMs, suggesting that perhaps they assumed that "a woman's desire to be a man is natural."[85] Although his focus on natal women set him apart from his contemporaries, his conclusion about the cause of gender nonconformity was quite familiar: moms of FTMs have a need to maintain "infantile omnipotence, arrogance and superiority," and they push "their daughters away from feminine identifications." He further argued that the daughters might take on male identifications "to ward off both theirs and their mothers' murderous wishes toward each other."[86]

A decade later, George Rekers, a psychologist and a right-wing Southern Baptist minister, was an even more strident voice. His *Handbook of Child and Adolescent Sexual Problems* discounted biological causes for gender nonconformity, placing blame squarely upon parents.[87] Rekers writes in a tone that suggests that he is simply reporting facts about the research of others, but his biases are apparent when he calls same-sex attractions "deviant patterns of sexual arousal."[88] He dismisses clinicians who disagree with his conclusions as promoting their personal and political agendas and represents his own position, in contrast, as totally objective and scientific—thus true.

Offering a slightly different explanation, Susan Coates, founder of the Parent-Infant Program at The Columbia Center for Psychoanalytic Training and Research, sees the feminine boy's trauma stemming from separation anxiety from the mother rather than from an over-strong aversion or connection to mom. The problem here is that the boy conflates "being mommy" with "having mommy."[89]

Following in the steps of those who came before them, Kenneth J. Zucker and Susan Bradley, also see the mother as the cause of GID. According to Zucker and Bradley, the parents' inability to set limits on the child, particularly regarding cross-gender behavior, creates anxiety for the child. GID develops when the relationships within the family allow the child to develop cross-gender behavior and opposite-sex identification. Zucker and Bradley stress that these factors must occur at a critical point of development for the child: when s/he is developing a coherent sense of self as male or female. They also note that GID-identified children tend to come from families with multiple clinical issues,[90] suggesting that trans kids are the products of dysfunctional families.

The researchers mentioned above are not isolated examples. Molly Ladd-Taylor, a historian at York University, examined academic journals from 1970, 1976, and 1982, and found 125 papers that blamed mothers for "seventy-two different kinds of problems in their offspring, ranging from bed-wetting to aggressive behavior, from learning problems to 'homicidal transsexualism.'"[91]

After reading these explanations of how a child comes to develop GID, I attempted to square them with the parents that I had interviewed. Of course, among them were some very assertive women who were determined to protect their child. That is certainly an accurate description of Karen as well, but it also happens to describe most mothers that I know whether or not their child is gender-nonconforming. Of course, I am not capable of and did not perform a psychological evaluation of the mothers that I interviewed, but they certainly did not come across as smothering, distant or murderous. Regarding the fathers, yes, some were out of the picture, but the majority of the families that I spoke to were intact, with the father not only present but actively engaged with and supportive of the child.

If not Mom, Who Do We Blame?

Prior to Freud, mothers were not generally assumed to be the creators of gender nonconformity in their children. In fact, prior to the creation of psychology, *why* people varied was not considered as important a question as what to do about these misfits. The problem was seen as a legal issue with the outcome being decided by a judge, not a doctor, and the decisions made were not always as hidebound as we might assume. For example, in Renaissance England, court rulings allowed latitude for transgender people, the restriction being that they should present themselves as the "sex that prevaileth."[92]

Voices of opposition to the strict reading of gender behavior and the blame game that accompanies it have not enjoyed the same level of exposure as Wylie and Strecker and those who followed them. As early as 1935, Margaret Mead provided evidence that gender roles are culturally defined, and that the roles of aggressor-hunter-logician man and the submitter-gatherer-emoter woman are not universal.[93] She argued that gender roles are malleable and differ among cultures, but once they are fixed within a culture they become a part of that culture's reality and occur to people in that culture as natural and unchanging.[94] Internationally renowned sociologist, Erving Goffman, called the entire idea of sex-linked behavior into question, arguing that the women's movement in America could be seen as doing more to weaken "doctrinal beliefs" about gender roles than to improve the lot of women. He questioned the necessity of distinctions between male and female behavior.[95]

In the mid-1960s, Milton Diamond challenged Money's assumption of environmental determination of gender identity, arguing that the *in utero* hormonal bath was a key determining factor.[96] The research to support the argument that *in utero* hormone levels predict gender identity is based upon assumptions that originate from the fact that hormones were discovered at the turn of the twentieth century. Biologists had known for centuries that sexual development and behavior was related to our gonads, but it wasn't until the late 1800s that they discovered that the way that gonads acted on the body was through the secretion of chemicals into the bloodstream.

Had this discovery happened at another point in history, we might not assume that there is such a thing as "sex" hormones, but the discovery occurred when sex and gender were foremost in the thinking of scientists. As biologist, Ruth Hubbard, argues, our approach to sex and the separation of genders hails from the fact that the theories of Darwin and Freud gained prominence at the same time. Concentrating on reproduction, Darwin was intent upon the separation of the aggressive male from the come-hither female, and Freud underscored that separation, arguing that we either suffer from the Oedipus Complex or penis envy:[97] take your pick, but you must choose between the two. As a result, turn-of-the century researchers wrote of testosterone and estrogen in terms reminiscent of the "battle of the sexes" that suggested that the hormones were pitted against each other for control of sex-typed development not only in the rodents and birds that were the focus of their experiments but in human beings as well. From their perspective, researchers believed that testosterone inhibited female development or that the two hormones functioned as antagonists, fighting each other for control of the body.[98] This mind-set has held such sway that it is still widely believed that prenatal hormones determine gender identity as well as sexual orientation. Even though ongoing research has shown that essentially every organ and biological system in the body respond to testosterone and estrogen in highly complex ways, we still think of these hormones only in terms of sex.[99]

The separation of testosterone as the male hormone and estrogen as the female hormone flies in the face of two important developments. First, in 1934, it was discovered that a stallion, the penultimate symbol of masculinity, has massive amounts of estrogen coursing through its veins. Second, four decades later, biochemists discovered that testosterone's effect on brain development usually takes place only after an enzyme in the brain transforms it into estrogen.[100] The bottom line: although there is no reason to doubt that prenatal hormone levels affect development, including gender identity, we have no clear evidence regarding how or to what extent they do so. The debate is not likely to subside any time soon.[101]

What about the brain, though? Have genes or prenatal hormones shaped the brains of trans children so that they are noticeably different? As with hormone research, the popular press tends to drastically simplify findings. In exploring "gendered" brains, scientists originally focused on the corpus callosum, a bundle of nerves that connects the right and left hemispheres of the brain. In 1982, after examining the corpus callosum of nine male brains and five female brains, two researchers published a two-page article in which they claimed that their findings "could be related to possible gender differences in the degree of lateral and visiospatial functions,"[102] which means that it is possible but not certain that male brains and female brains process visual-spatial information differently. This conclusion was drawn from the fact that among the few brains that they had examined, parts of the corpus callosum of the male brain seemed to be smaller than that of the female brain. Although the report merely suggested that there might be a difference in the way that male and female brains function, the media reported the research as showing that men were missing a part of their brains.[103]

Subsequent research has shown differences between male and female brains in limited numbers of post-mortem studies, which have focused on sections of the hypothalamus and the amygdala. The most striking results come from a Dutch team which has seen evidence that parts of the brains of trans women appear to be female in structure.[104] These results are preliminary and very limited, and, despite what might be reported in the mass media about these studies, they certainly do not mean that we have found any clear evidence of what causes gender nonconformity. In order to actually understand the answers that science provides, we need to guard against the tendency to simplify evidence that is complex and inconclusive.

Phyllis Burke reminds us of our tendency to overstate and over-simplify the differences in behavior between genders, pointing out that in the United States, as in most cultures, it is perfectly acceptable to think of gender as an absolute, breaking people into two simple categories and making global assumptions about their behaviors and abilities. As a result, a girl who is good at math might be seen as having a "male" brain and a boy who plays with dolls might be seen as having a "female" brain.[105]

Aside from the oversimplifications that surround us in popular culture and the media, research methods used to draw conclusions about brain function have their own limitations. Current technology limits the ways in which we can examine the brain. We can dissect cadavers, slicing off portions of the brain and examining them micro-scopically or we can examine the brains of living subjects through MRIs or the use of sensors to detect blood flow or electrical impulses. Each of these approaches has shortcomings that cloud any conclusions drawn from the research.[106]

While we are on the subject of oversimplification, let's consider the foundation of the entire debate: nature v. nurture. Reminiscent of the prevalent assumption that testosterone and estrogen battle to control the body and mind, we are once again boxed in—this time by the belief that everything about our child, every trait and every behavior, is the result of nature or nurture—nurture if we like what we see, nature if we don't. Our child is generous and caring because she was well-raised, but she is moody and brooding only because of her bloodline, which, of course, we parents can't control. If pressed, we might announce ourselves to be open-minded and accept that a given trait or behavior *might* be some combination of both.

Where did this paradigm come from? Is it a valid means of measuring human development and behavior?

It turns out that the division of nature and nurture originated in the 1870s with Francis Galton, a cousin of Charles Darwin, and is central to most of psychology. It is certainly central to psychological theories regarding gender nonconformity, and treatment regimens are affected by a therapist's assumptions. If the assumption is that gender nonconformity is innate (stemming from nature), it makes sense to help the client find ways to cope with the condition or counteract its effect. If it is assumed to be a conditioned response (stemming from nurture), treatment logically focuses on helping the client find ways to correct the problem behavior. At present, there is a considerably heated debate about proper treatment, with theorists who hold entrenched positions arguing that the treatment protocol of those who oppose their views amounts to abuse of the client.[107]

Galton's paradigm has had considerable staying power even though many people have pointed out its obvious flaws.[108] To be valid, an either-or supposition needs to answer two tests: Are the two options mutually exclusive? Do the two options represent all possible choices?[109]

Galton's paradigm does not hold up to either test. Upon examination, it becomes apparent that, far from being mutually exclusive, nature (genes) and nurture (environment) are inseparable. Left on its own, DNA is essentially inert and its genetic code cannot "compute" a result without interacting with its environment at the cellular level.[110] Furthermore, adaptations to the environment can create significant biological changes that would appear to require genetic coding in order to exist, one example being a goat that was born without front legs and spent its life hopping around on its hind legs. An autopsy showed that it had developed a human-shaped spine and other anatomical features related to walking erect.[111] Regarding gender, biologist Ruth Hubbard put it this way:

> . . . being raised as a boy or a girl produces biological as well as social differences. Society defines the sex-appropriate behavior to which each of us learns to conform, and our behavior affects our bones, muscles, sense organs, nerves, brain, lungs, circulation, everything. In this way society constructs us as biologically, as well as socially, gendered people. It does not give us a vagina or a penis, but it helps give us the muscles, gait, body language, and nervous responses that we associate with people who are born with one or the other.[112]

For example, even if we can point to a particular part of the brain that is different in men than in women, we cannot logically assume that the difference is genetically mandated. Galton fails test one.

How about test two? Are there really any other options? Arguments that indeed there are other options have been made since at least the 1980s. Harvard biologist, Richard C. Lewontin, has presented a case regarding this point, at least partially in response to the Human Genome Project.[113] His book, *The Triple Helix* warns against the assumption that nature and nurture account for all traits and behavior, pointing out that what we think of as evolutionary changes amount to the adaptations or choices that organisms (read our children) make on a minute-to-minute basis in response to challenges from the environment. He reminds his reader that the environment and the organism evolve together, each having an impact on the other. He and others note that these choices happen at the level of *organism*, not of the cell.[114]

In other words, when we attempt to understand our child's behavior as the result only of nature, nurture or some combination of the two, we deny our child any free will. These are our children, not lumps of clay that have been molded by the whim of genetic coding and environment. They are living, thinking beings, and every parent knows from personal experience that a child resists being molded by parental whim. If parenting were only that simple! That is not to say that our children "choose" to be gender-nonconforming. If they find the gender roles offered to them to be repugnant, they respond in ways that work for them. A girl hates skirts and loves rough-and-tumble play, so she chooses to play with others who are like-minded. Given the way that children are socialized, is it any surprise that her like-minded playmates are all boys? Given the way that we use comparisons to others to define ourselves, is it any surprise that this girl feels more comfortable being "one of the guys" than being laughed at and branded a tomboy by the others on the playground?

Getting Past "Why?"

Let me share a totally unresearched hypothesis. Have you ever had a three-year old ask, 'Why?' so many times that you end up saying, "Because I said so"? I believe that we find that repeated "Why?" frustrating because it is an echo of the question that drives our thinking throughout life. Rather than being satisfied with allowing things (and people) simply to be, we have a deep-seated need to make sense of what happens around us and to us. It's almost as if we never get past being three and asking that question. We will expend no end of mental effort to answer the question, even when it focuses on a mildly perplexing behavior such as "Why did she smile at me that way?" When the stakes are high, and the situation has a significant effect on us or those close to us, the need to answer that question can become torturous.

I have never spoken to the parent of a gender-nonconforming child who does not want the answer to why, and the drive to find the answer is understandable because our child's difference is seen not only as a shame but also shameful, and we are blamed by ourselves as well as others. Mothers in particular must face the blunt accusations that began early in the history of psychology in the United States and still reverberate today, not just in the popular press but also in scholarly journals. So it is no wonder that we think such thoughts as "What did I do wrong," "Please, don't let it be me" "It can't be me" and "It must be something else." When we are forced into such a defensive mind-set, we fall back on our three-year-old thinking that looks for a simple answer, and simple answers can be derived only from asking simple, mindless questions such as "Is it nature or nurture?"

The either-or trap is enticing because it helps us to avoid uncertainty by reducing any issue to the most basic simplicity, which makes a complex problem appear to be immediately comprehensible—but comprehensible only at the most remedial, and inaccurate level. When we reduce our intelligence to either-or thinking, we no longer have to consider the irritating tangle of multiple possibilities that confront us because we have boiled down the daunting enigma to two options. Once we choose one of those options, the crisis of uncertainty is over and we can ignore the complexities involved. This child-like thinking is quite prevalent today. Look at the stark polarity of our national conversation: are you conservative or liberal, a Republican or a Democrat, from a red state or a blue state, with us or against us. The trouble with such facile thinking is that it leaves no room for real exploration of problems because it rules out the variations, nuances and possibilities that adults need to accept and be willing to wrestle with. Three-year-old thinking is not going to cut it.

So we're stuck with no answer, at least for now, and possibly forever. Perhaps we would benefit by falling back to a perspective reminiscent of Renaissance England. Why not give "Why?" a rest so that we can focus on what is to be done?

CHAPTER 5

Learning about and Dealing with What Is Coming Your Way

"So what are we in for? Where is this all going?"
"Does this mean surgery?"
"Now what? I just don't know what to expect.

AFTER CADENCE CAME OUT TO us, Karen and I were asking ourselves all three of the questions above along with countless others. I would like to have pretended that I had a clue about what was going on, but since I knew couldn't pull that off, I simply accepted that I was lost. In a way, though I was relieved: at least there was now an explanation for the depression that she had suffered since shortly after starting college. Of course, I knew that Cadence's issues with gender weren't necessarily the cause of the depression. In fact, there was a good deal of evidence to suggest that the depression preceded her awareness of gender nonconformity by several years. Still, I now had something to pin it all on, and I could always claim that there was no way to prove that gender confusion (or whatever we were supposed to call it) *wasn't* at the root of the problem. But, aside from the occasional article or book in my efforts at research, I wasn't finding many answers.

There is standing joke in the gay culture that once a kid comes out of the closet, the parents go in. Like many jokes, this one is funny because it is has the ring of truth. Most of the people in our lives were very supportive, but, looking back at how I handled the situation, I clearly was not comfortable with it. I kept opening my closet door a bit then closing it again.

It's no secret that college faculty tend to be rather liberal in their thinking, and since it was safe to do so, I came out to co-workers shortly after I accepted that Cadence wasn't going to change her mind. However, as I revealed in chapter three, I did not come out to my family for nearly three years for fear of rejection. Even though my family had always been very loving and supportive, I feared that they would not understand. Of course, I know now that my reticence is a normal, predictable stage of the process that we go through.

Stage Models of the Family Process

There are several models that break down the experience of transsexualism into stages, but most of them focus on the gender-nonconforming individual, not the family.[115] There are, however, three published models that attempt to explain the family's experience: Shirley Emerson and Carole Rosenfeld (1996), Kelly Ellis and Karen Eriksen (2002) and Arlene Lev and Laura Alie (2012). I offer below an outline for each of these models.

Keep in mind that none of these models argues that a family (or any individual in the family) marches through the stages in lock-step fashion. Just as Elisabeth Kübler-Ross noted in *On Death and Dying*, we may seem to skip some stages or might be quite far along with certain aspects of the process but just getting started with another. One father, for example, has no issue with being out to family and friends and always uses female pronouns when talking about his adult trans daughter, but he still struggles with her choices in apparel and is startled when he sees his "son" in a skirt. It is also possible for a family or an individual member to relapse to an earlier stage. Rather than thinking of the stages as steps on staircase that we are climbing, it us useful to think of them as a progression of traffic signs on a road trip. There is bound to be more than one sharp turn on the journey, and since our map has no detail, we should expect to get lost along the way and end up back-tracking or taking a few detours. As we examine the three models, you will notice that they overlap each other at points, but each one offers useful insights.

Emerson and Rosenfeld were the first to examine how families adapt to the discovery of gender nonconformity.[116] Their five stages directly mirror those identified by Kübler-Ross: (1) Denial, (2) Anger, (3) Bargaining, (4) Depression, and (5) Acceptance.

A family may maintain the **denial** stage for an extended period of time, especially if the gender-nonconforming member is not present. If family members disagree about how (or whether) to support the gender nonconformity, it may be more comfortable to stay in denial than to confront the disagreement. During this stage, families may think that the trans member is "going through a phase," a belief that family members may cling to even if the trans member is fifty years old and has fully transitioned. The **anger** phase may result in the trans member being blamed for all the family's problems, and members may feel betrayed, wondering what other dark secrets have been kept. During the **bargaining** phase, the family may threaten to disown or may collaborate to shun the trans member. They may offer bribes in an effort to "normalize" behavior. If the family has a history of being secretive, they may even insist that the trans member keep surgery or behavior a secret. Such a family is likely to find it exceptionally difficult to accept changes. Once the transgenderism is no longer deniable or able to be bargained away, family members may suffer from **depression**, expressing grief over loss, suffering physical illness or substance abuse. This may draw attention away from the trans member and allow the family to focus on the needs of other members. The family reaches **acceptance** when it no longer seeks to "correct" the behavior. Although they may not agree with the behavior or decisions made by the trans member, they begin to show concerns for the trans member's welfare, health and the issues faced with employment or relationships.

Ellis and Eriksen break the process into the following six stages: (1) Shock and Denial, (2) Anger and Fear, (3) Seeking Support, (4) Self-Discovery, (5) Acceptance, and (6) Pride.[117]

In stage one, the parents are in such **shock** that they may exhibit symptoms similar to those encountered with post traumatic stress. They may exhibit **denial** by expecting the gender nonconformity is just a phase that will dissipate, or they may offer partial acceptance by making it "okay for Jackie to be a girl and not get married or have children [or] okay for her to be a girl and not wear dresses or makeup."[118] What is *not* okay is for Jackie to insist that she is really Jack. Parents who remain at this stage for an extended period of time may undermine their child's self-esteem. During the **anger** stage, parents may become angry at the child for subjecting them to this ordeal or for a perceived loss of the child or future grandchildren. They may feel guilt about being inadequate parents or rejected because the child does not want to be like them. They also worry about the impact on siblings and rejection from family and friends. As for **fear**, the worry about social stigma can be quite acute and may create shame, and it is possible that they may even avoid talking to the trans child during this stage for fear of saying the wrong thing. Counseling can be of particular help here to bring these feelings out in the open so that they can be dealt with.

In stage three, **seeking support**, parents talk with others and attempt to learn more. They benefit from interacting with other parents with similar experiences. Working with support groups such as PFLAG may be especially helpful during this stage, because parents may experience considerable cognitive dissonance, knowing that their child's gender nonconformity is not just a "stage" but still being in denial about the process.

As they become more knowledgeable, parents progress toward **self-discovery**. They begin to reexamine societal assumptions about gender and may be confronted by their own prejudices about gender and sexuality. Their thinking about gender becomes more flexible, but they may find that they do not agree with the gender expression of the child.

Acceptance emerges when the parents are able to witness their child's happiness in the new gender. They often become "co-conspirators" with their child to overcome obstacles at school, at work, or in relationships. Some report relief that "we finally have our kid back" or feel that the process has created stronger family bonds and deeper understanding among members.

Finally, the parents may find themselves **taking pride** in their child's courage to confront such a daunting challenge. They may see themselves as having a stronger sense of self, a greater acceptance of themselves and others. They may eventually become advocates—working to move organizations or other people to greater understanding.[119]

Lev and Alie's stages are (1) Discovery and Disclosure, (2) Turmoil, (3) Negotiation, (4) Finding Balance.[120] In the first stage, when they either **discover** the gender nonconformity in their child or have it **disclosed** to them, parents may be relatively accepting, especially if the child is young, and they may wonder if the child is gay. Some parents may advocate for their child but others may be shocked by the revelation, especially if it conflicts with religious views. As demonstrated in chapter one, even when we are aware of the gender issue, the realization of its importance or prominence in our child's life can be quite upsetting.

Although not all families experience stage two, **turmoil**, it is often a time of intense stress and conflict within the family. Parents may have differing views and some members of the family may be supportive while others are outraged or in denial, the result being that sides are chosen. Stress is often particularly high by questions of physical transition.

Stage three is a time of **negotiation** for family members as they realize that the gender issues will not vanish and must be adjusted to in some manner. Families begin to engage in a process of compromise, determining what they are comfortable with regarding transition issues and what limits the family will set with gender expression. This is akin to Ellis and Eriksen's **self-discovery** stage.

Reaching the final stage, **finding balance**, does not necessarily suggest formal transition to the other sex nor does it mean permanent resolution of gender issues. It means that the gender nonconformity is no longer a secret and that the family has negotiated the larger issues involving transgenderism. The family has learned that there is a difference between secrecy and privacy and is now ready to integrate the gender nonconformity into its sense of "normal" family interaction. It is not unusual for the family to find themselves content in their daily interactions.

Stages—Schmages. How Do I Get through the Next Five Minutes?

Although it's great to have a better understanding of the process that we are working through, what do you do if your kid's not speaking to you today? Without exception, the families that I have spoken to have experienced breakdowns at several points along their journey. Those breakdowns may be between you and your child, between you and your spouse, between your child and siblings, between your immediate family and the extended family, or between you and friends. There seems to be no limit to number or size of the potholes on this road, so it's worthwhile to have some strategies on hand to deal with moments of tension or crisis. Let's look first at your interactions with your child.

Regardless of the child's age, certain approaches are likely to provide positive outcomes and others are almost assured to provide more turmoil and bruised egos. Most of what I share in the rest of the chapter is based upon theories that have a proven track record, but I'll start with an approach offered by a grandfather of a trans woman. There had been some rocky moments in the relationship after his trans granddaughter came out, but they had always been close. After they had worked their way through some challenging confrontations, he simply asked, "Do I have anything to apologize for?" This is a question to be asked at a moment when nerves are calm, not in the heat of a pitched battle. It invites your child to reflect on any actions or words that have been hurtful while you fumbled through this difficult process. Of course, you must be prepared to accept the answer, which means that you must be open to receive the perspective offered.

Let's say that you child says, "Yes, when you screwed up pronouns and my name during the family dinner at Grandma's." What do you say next? One clue: don't say, "Well, I was still getting used to all that" or "I'm not the only one who did that." Remember, you did not start this conversation by asking, "Is there anything that you want to hear me justify?"

Instead of mounting a defense, actually apologize—listen to the criticism or complaint, find an aspect of it that you can agree with, and acknowledge your part in the situation. It also helps if you indicate that you can see why the apology is needed. You might say, "Yes, I did do that, and I am sorry that I did. It must have been humiliating for you." This approach is called *agreeing with the critic*,[121] and it can be an effective means of clarifying and defusing past actions.

If you do not hear something that you can agree with, ask for specifics to get more information. If nothing else, you can certainly agree with the perception offered you.

Child: You don't listen to me.

Parent: I'm sorry. Can you give me an example?

Child: I told you yesterday that I want to be in Nilda's wedding but I don't want to wear a dress.

Parent: Yes, I remember that.

Child: But you didn't call her to straighten it out.

Parent: Oh, you thought I was going to call her! I can see why that would upset you.

Notice that the parent is not yet offering to take any action but is helping the child to explore what has been bothering him. The point is to provide acknowledgement and confirmation. By continuing this process until you have explored all the moments in which your behavior has been hurtful to your child, you can help her/him feel accepted and fully heard, perhaps for the first time.

Of course, holding yourself back from justifying past actions can be difficult because, rather than acknowledge our failings and accept responsibility for them, we prefer to think of ourselves as sensitive and effective communicators even though we may have never received any instruction in effective communication. When someone criticizes us—even with our permission or encouragement—it may feel as if we are being attacked. So we become defensive, which provokes a defensive response in those around us and creates a climate that shuts down openness and acceptance, the very qualities that we most need to work through difficult situations with our loved ones.

Jack Gibb, a Stanford psychologist, developed a powerful model that helps to address these issues. In studying groups, Gibb determined that there are six behaviors that establish whether the communication climate is supportive or defensive.[122] To provide the supportive climate that you and your gender-nonconforming child need to get through the challenges that you will both face, you need to keep your behavior and words on the right side to the chart below. As we'll see from the discussion that follows, *understanding* what would be helpful for the relationship is far easier than *doing* what needs to be done. It might be more accurate to label the left column as "Normal" rather than "Defensive."

Gibb's Chart of Supportive and Defensive Behaviors

Defensive	Supportive
Evaluation	Description
Control	Problem Orientation
Superiority	Equality
Neutrality	Empathy
Strategy	Spontaneity
Certainty	Provisionalism

Evaluation v. Description

We tend to collapse the meaning that we assign to an event with what actually happened, the result being that the meaning we invented feels as "true" to us as the event itself. Let's return to Rhonda, who we met in the first chapter. No doubt she had reason to be shocked when her son, Casey, came out as transgender in a local newspaper article and claimed that she had kicked him out of the house because he was trans. When someone does something like that, the first question we ask is "Why?" Our answer includes the evaluation that we assign to the action. If Rhonda focuses on her evaluation, she would say that Casey was being spiteful and was attacking her in public, but if she were to describe what actually occurred, she'd say that Casey agreed to an interview and the paper published an article that misrepresented what had happened. It can be extremely difficult to rid your communication of evaluation, but it helps if you consciously work to avoid any interpretation of the behavior that you describe. When you accurately describe *what* happened, you report facts. When you explain *why* it happened, you assign motives. Bottom line: don't assign motives for others actions. Here are a few examples:

Evaluation	Description
So, you're just walking out on this conversation?	When I said that, you turned and walked away.
You should show us some respect.	We haven't heard from you in two weeks, and we worry when that happens.

Control v. Problem Orientation

It can also be difficult to be problem-oriented rather than controlling, especially if our child is a minor. We are, of course, morally and legally obligated to "control" the behavior of a minor who is under our care. But it is no secret to parents that children resist control from an early age. If you find that you are dictating a course of action rather than exploring it, you are controlling you child and provoking resistance and defensiveness. "You are not leaving the house looking like that!" is sure to spark a battle because it assumes that you have total control of your child. To be problem-oriented, explore the issue at hand. Your eight-year-old son wants to walk to Josh's house wearing his big sister's shorts and pink blouse. A blunt NO! may be understandable to you, but it tells him that *he* has no control.

First, ask yourself to identify the problem. Are you concerned for his safety or that he'll be teased? Or are you concerned that *you* will be embarrassed? You might say, "If you go outside like that, the neighborhood kids might make fun of you like last week. Do you remember?" Doing so focuses him on the issue rather forcing your solution to the issue on him. His answer also might provide you with insights into what he is thinking and feeling, insights you will not tap into with a blunt refusal.

Superiority v. Equality

Behaviors that control others are the behaviors of a superior. Of course, if your child is a fourteen-year-old, she is clearly not your equal. That does not mean, however, that communication with her should reinforce that fact. On the other hand, if your child is forty-five, you are no longer her superior, and behaving as if you are is certain to create friction. Interacting with your child as an equal does not mean that you surrender all power in the relationship. Instead it acknowledges the child's as valued and invites the child to provide her point of view. The result is that she feels respected and more willing to cooperate. If she feels that she is being treated as an equal, she is more likely to focus on working with you to solve a problem than if she feels that you are dictating her behavior to her. Consider the following examples:

Superiority	Equality
You are not going to lay this on your grandmother right now. She doesn't need to know yet.	I worry about how Grandma might take this! I'd like to talk through how and when to approach her.
If you get back late, you're grounded for a month.	Remember that we agreed on midnight. I can't help but worry when you come in late.

The second example might seem as if the mother is "being soft," but she has not backed off the agreement. Instead, she has offered a reminder yet provided evidence that she respects the child's ability to control her own behavior. In contrast, the parent who uses "do-this-or-you'll-get-that" ultimatums, has already set a defensive tone because she is emphasizing her power to punish.

The practice of equality can be a daunting challenge in a parent-child relationship, especially if it has not been part of a family's behavioral pattern. It is worthwhile to step outside yourself and reflect on the way that you interact with your child to consider whether statements expressing equality might be so foreign as to arouse suspicions, causing your child to question your sincerity. If that is the case, consider approaching the process transparently by admitting the role you have played. After reflection, if you sense that your child experiences you as dictatorial and overbearing, it does you no good to dismiss her perception as inaccurate or immature. You might try saying something like this: "I know that I may come off as bossy, but I want us to overcome challenges together.

We're facing some big issues now, and we'll need to work as a team to deal with them. So I'm hoping that you'll see that I'm working to be a good teammate."

Your child needs to know that you are working with her, not on her.

Strategy v. Spontaneity[123]

Strategy has to do with hiding your motives or engaging in manipulation. If you have had counseling and your child senses that you are "using techniques" suggested by the counselor, you are likely to get a defensive response. You may also provoke a confrontation when you make it seem that your child is making a choice when you are actually steering the choice in a particular direction. On the other hand, spontaneous interaction is open and free of such deception. To put this in perspective, imagine that you are at lunch with a friend, and twenty minutes into the conversation your friend casually mentions a great way to make money on the Internet. At that moment you realize the entire event has been staged so that your friend could pitch you on this opportunity. That's strategic manipulation. Here are examples from family situations:

Strategy	Spontaneity
Have you considered what could happen if you do that?	I'm not comfortable with you going to a party in such a remote location.
Becky keeps us posted on what's going on in her life.	We'd like to hear from you more often.

As seen in the first example above, rather than masking the parent's position, the spontaneous statement openly displays that position so that the child understands the reason for the objection. The strategic statement in the second example inserts a sense of competition with the sister that masks the real concern, which is an appeal for more contact.

Neutrality v. Empathy

Neutrality suggests a lack of concern or involvement for family members, which makes them feel unloved and unvalued. When issues between siblings arise, parents understandably avoid choosing sides, but maintaining a neutral stance provides support for neither child. In contrast, empathy demonstrates a concern for both children and an understanding of their feelings. Although this may seem to be a challenge, it usually is not that difficult for a parent to put himself in his child's place. It is important not to substitute sympathy for empathy—feeling sorry for someone keeps you at an emotional distance, but understanding and embracing how they feel provides acceptance and nurturance. Consider the following examples:

Neutrality	Empathy
I'm not getting involved. Work it out with your sister.	Wow, that must make you feel like she's taking advantage of you.
Don't get so upset. Sometimes we lose friends, that's all.	That must really hurt. Nobody likes to be betrayed like that.
Sorry, but I have to get to work. Maybe we can talk later, okay?	I'm running late this morning, but I can see that you want to talk. How about if I take you to lunch so we can discuss it?

Certainty v. Provisionalism

We all have known someone who is always right and is not satisfied until he has proven everyone else wrong. Such dogmatic insistence is what Gibb referred to as certainty. Since certain statements leave no room for discussion or compromise, they belittle others by dismissing their points of view as worthless. In contrast, provisional statements allow room for exploration and may even invite contradiction. The person who is provisional still has opinions, even very pointed ones, but she expresses them in a way that allows others to challenge her assumptions or share their thinking without fear of being shouted down or attacked.

Certainty	Provisionalism
Trust me. That never works with her. She's going to really let you have it.	Do you think it would work if you were less direct?
Seeing her has been a waste of time.	As I see it, we haven't gotten much out of those sessions. What do you think?

You may have noticed a pattern in the examples above. The vast majority of defensive responses contain the pronoun *you* and the supportive ones contain the pronouns *I* or *we*. We use *you* for accusations such as "You never listen to me" or for commands such as "You need to pay attention." When pressed or upset, we shorten these to even more abrupt commands: "Listen to me. Pay attention!" *You* statements show a lack of respect for the other person's needs and come off as aggressive.[124] We can defuse emotions for both us and for the person we are upset with by simply rephrasing an objection so that it starts with *I* or *we*: "I'm upset because it feels like you don't listen to me" or "I need to have your attention."

"I" statements are assertive: they clearly express what we want or need and also demonstrate respect for the other person, but they are not a new idea and can register as manipulative if they sound artificial. To avoid antagonism, don't sugar-coat emotions, but describe your feelings in words that suggest distress (frustrated, anxious, worried, hurt) rather than words that suggest anger (annoyed, resentful, mad, pissed off). It is even worthwhile to consciously *think* in "I" statements. When your child—or anyone—does something that strikes you as outrageous, pay attention to what you are thinking. If you find yourself responding with a thought like, "You obnoxious brat!" take note and consider how you can rephrase your thinking: "I'm getting worked up here; I'm letting myself get rattled." Remember that starting from *I* allows you to reassert to yourself that it is possible to choose how you respond to any situation. Of course, as with any of the suggestions in this chapter, we become proficient at *I* language only through ongoing practice.

Conflict: Dealing with Negative or Confrontational Situations

Despite efforts to maintain a supportive climate, there will certainly be moments of conflict, and most of us harbor negative assumptions about conflict based on negative results in the past. We know from experience that conflict has the potential to create rifts and poison relationships. Certainly not all conflicts can be resolved and some are best left unaddressed, but it is our management of conflict, not the conflict itself, which creates the result. Although potentially destructive, conflict can help to clarify our thinking and our values, and it can even create greater closeness and intimacy. All of us have had the experience of working our way through a conflict with someone to find that we have a greater appreciation and love for the person whose neck we wanted to ring yesterday.

Since the process that trans families go through is fraught with conflicts—between parent and child, between siblings, between parents, between immediate and extended family—let's take a systematic look at conflict management. First, we'll consider how significant or important the conflict is, then we'll consider the best means of addressing the conflict, and finally, we'll look at a specific method of managing the most important conflicts that you might face.

One means of determining the importance and nature of a conflict is to measure the needs of the parties involved. What needs do you have at stake and how important is it to you to have them met? What needs does the other person have at stake and how important is it to you that those needs are met? When approached in this way, we often find that a conflict that seems significant is not actually putting anyone's needs at stake, which means it's not a conflict at all, just a momentary annoyance. Imagine that you are sitting at a red light, and the second the light turns green, the driver behind you lays on the horn. Perhaps you find your blood boiling or you feel an urge to offer your horn-happy fellow motorist a blunt salute. But if we examine the incident in terms of needs, we see how silly—or at least how illogical—such a response is because no significant needs are at stake. We have an irritation, not a conflict. Of course, not all situations that upset us are innocuous, and many of them do put important needs at stake. The graph below, based on work by Kenneth Thomas in the 1970s, provides guidance in sorting out what type of response is appropriate for a given conflict.[125]

Responses to Conflict Based upon Needs-Analysis

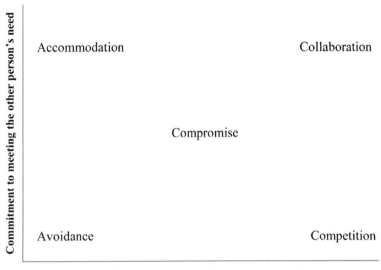

Most of us have a default means of dealing with conflict. When we face conflict, we fall into a familiar pattern of behavior. Many people, sensing danger or unpleasantness, simply avoid the conflict. They put off doing or saying anything in the hope that the conflict will somehow disappear. If that does not work, these people may simply cave in, allowing the other person to have his way. In other words they accommodate the other person.

Perhaps, though, you gravitate toward the opposite extreme, insisting upon getting your way. In that case, your knee-jerk response to the beeping horn might be to offer your fellow motorist that salute and then to pull ever so slowly into the intersection. If so, you are generally competitive and you like to win when faced with conflict.

The graph is intended to help us make a conscious choice when faced with conflict rather than simply falling back to our default response. It's easy to follow our default pattern and not even recognize that we are making a choice. Not recognizing our response as a choice does not mean, however, that no choice has been made. Lashing out is a choice. Getting even is a choice. So is walking away or stopping to consider how to respond. Thomas argues that to deal with the conflict productively we should match our response to the needs at stake in the conflict. The more we sense our needs are at stake and need to be met, the more appropriate it is to compete; and the more the needs of the other person are at stake and should be met, the more appropriate it is to accommodate.

Let's look at a few examples to see how the graph works. One couple that I interviewed had an elderly Aunt Mildred who simply would not accept the transition of Jeff, their adult FTM, and refused to use male pronouns or his chosen name. Aunt Mildred said, "I refuse to see her unless she is properly dressed, and I don't want to hear any more about it." Aunt Mildred lived in a neighboring state, the couple saw her perhaps once a year, and she had seen Jeff only twice in the ten years since his high school graduation—at a funeral and at a wedding. Her rigidness was upsetting, but they saw no way to address the situation, so they did nothing. If we consider Thomas's approach to managing conflict, we can see that they decided to avoid the conflict. The aunt had expressed a strong desire not to hear about this, and they had no meaningful needs at stake. Her relationship with Jeff was not significant, and it was likely that the two would seldom cross paths if at all. They also accommodated Aunt Mildred's request that she hear no more about the issue. If there is another family gathering that both Jeff and Aunt Mildred will attend, there might be moment or two of awkwardness during the event, but the two need not interact directly.

There are, though, situations that call for a stronger response, such as this one: Sally's family lives in Wisconsin, and her sixteen-year-old FTM, Landon, has been out as trans in his high school for two years. This past fall, there was a change in administration and a new principal took over. On multiple occasions, the new principal confronted Landon even pulling him in to a meeting with an assistant principal. In that meeting she explained that on a school trip to Minneapolis, Landon was not to use the public men's room and would be required to use the toilet on the bus. She also declared that she considered Landon's insistence upon using the male restrooms at the school a disciplinary issue.

Examining this situation from our model, it is clear that the principal's stance puts Landon's needs under attack. The family had negotiated an agreement with the previous administration regarding the use of restrooms, and under Minnesota law Landon is entitled to use whatever facility he chooses on the school trip. Sally did not see any reason to concern herself with the principal's needs, especially since Landon had been using the boys' facilities at school for two years without issue. Sally chose to compete. She contacted a lawyer with the ACLU who explained the law to the principal. She also contacted the school's superintendent, who had been consistently supportive of Landon's transition, to request that the harassment stop. The result: the principal has been told that she is not to interact further with Landon.

So far we have looked at three of the five methods of managing conflict. Since the incident with the horn-happy motorist rates low on both the scales, the appropriate means of management would be avoid conflict—just pull through the intersection and ignore the incident. The situation with Aunt Mildred comprised no risk to Jeff's or the family's needs, and accommodation was the most suitable course of action. Sally's choice to compete matched the situation because Landon's needs trumped the principal's concerns. Accommodation and competition are two sides of the same coin, and they have their limitations. Accommodation is a passive lose/win approach—you lose, the other person wins—whereas competition is an aggressive, win/lose approach—you win, the other person loses. When we are in conflict with people who are an important part of our lives, win/lose and lose/win choices aren't very appealing because we want to meet the other person's needs as well as our own. In such situations these strategies are inadequate because enough is at stake that we don't want to settle for compromise. Although, even with concerted effort, success is not guaranteed, the best choice in these situations is adopt a win/win approach: to collaborate, working together on the conflict so that everyone's needs are fully met.

Consider Sheila, a nineteen-year-old MTF who is home from college for the summer, and is eager to get on with her transition. She is engaged in a pitched battle with her parents because she has been using street hormones while away at college. She argues that the endocrinologist she has been seeing is too conservative and that she needs a higher hormone dosage to move her transition forward. She started college as a woman last fall, and is distressed with the lack of breast development. Barb and Phil feel that Sheila is in too much of a rush and insist that she follow the doctor's orders. Working with our model, we can see that Barb and Phil's central needs, Sheila's health and remaining in a relationship with her, are extremely important to them, but they cannot dismiss Sheila's needs because too much is at stake.[126] Their past attempts to restrict her access to hormones met with her making threats to leave and take her chances living on the street. To be successful, the resolution of this conflict must fulfill everyone's needs and that resolution in such a case is almost never immediately apparent, but it might be possible to find the resolution through a process called *principled negotiation*.[127]

The Three Components of Principled Negotiation

1. *Separate the People from the Problem*: focus attention and comments on the conflict.
2. *Focus on Interests, not Positions*: get to the core reasons behind the positions taken.
3. *Invent New Options for Mutual Gain*: keep an open mind, and don't get trapped into either-or thinking.

Separating the people from the problem: Barb and Phil are exasperated by Sheila's attitude. They feel that they have been very supportive and have put out a great deal of money to help Sheila. They even paid extra for her to have a single room at college to protect her privacy but no matter what they do, it never seems to be enough for Sheila. They have threatened to stop paying for college if they can't trust her while she is away from home. For her part, Sheila feels that her parents' focus on money is just a manipulative way to control her. She is angry that they can't seem to understand how difficult this is for her. She feels as if everyone looks at her like she's a freak. Nobody at the college has actually said anything to her, but her fear of being read is continuous. To separate the people from the problem, Sheila and her parents need to stop blaming each other and examine what is at issue in the conflict. They need to define the problem in terms of those issues rather than past actions. For Barb and Phil, the issue is safety. For Sheila, the issue is respect. If they can bring themselves to discuss the problem in terms of those issues—the conflict between the need for safety and the need for respect—they may gain the perspective needed to work on the problem.

Focusing on interests, not positions: By choosing to buy hormones off the street, Sheila has stated a clear position: I am going to get what I want even if you don't approve. By threatening to withhold payment to the college, Barb and Phil have also stated a position: do as we say or no college for you. If everyone stays focused on these positions, the conflict will continue to be framed as a competition: the only way to win is to assure that the other party loses. But if they work through the differences that they have by exploring *why* their positions are being taken, they have a chance to create a more productive discussion. The *reason* for Barb and Phil's position is that they are worried about Sheila's health and the dangers involved in altering her hormonal balance without proper medical supervision. The *reason* for Sheila's position is that she wants to move through her transition faster and that she is not being heard. If they can stay focused on the interests of health and being heard, they will frame the problem in terms that can be discussed with less emotion. Sheila can hardly deny the need to remain healthy, nor can Barb and Phil reasonably deny Sheila's sense of urgency or her right to be heard.

Inventing new options for mutual gain: Having separated themselves from the problem and gotten past positions to an examination of interests, Sheila, Barb and Phil have opened the door to choices and are no longer boxed into the mutually exclusive either-or battle that they have been fighting for weeks. Now that the conflict is defined as being about the need for healthy behavior and the need to be heard, the family can explore ways to address both needs. They can seek other opinions to see if the current endocrinologist is being too conservative. They can engage in family counseling to assure that Sheila feels more fully heard. They can agree to ask the therapist if she has any other endocrinologists that she might refer them to. They can also explore what support might be available for Sheila on campus. By working together to find ways that everyone's needs are met, they gain a better understanding not only of how to address this conflict but also of how they can more effectively work as a team to confront the other challenges that they will face as Sheila continues her transition.

Of course, choosing to engage in principled negotiation does not guarantee success. The process will be successful only if everyone works in good faith to make progress in resolving the conflict. Agreeing to proceed with the process does not make emotions less intense, issues less complex or positions less closed-minded. Yet with ongoing effort and an agreement to stay the course, we increase the odds that we will find a workable result. Given the heightened emotions, don't be surprised if there are outbreaks of hostility. It may even be you who becomes hostile because when the mood becomes combative we fall into the old pattern of feeling attacked and wanting to strike back. Let's take a look at one final model for managing such a moment.

Supportive Confrontation: Negotiating Rough Seas

Most of us avoid confrontation, perhaps because we associate it with stress, unpleasantness and emotional upheaval. When we have a confrontation with someone, we get upset. Not liking to be upset, we feel in that moment as if something must be wrong—the other person must be wrong or somehow we must be wrong—and we find a false sense of solace in placing blame. We might blame the other person for not being more sensitive to our needs or ourselves for somehow failing to keep the waters smooth.

Let's consider that metaphor. As the parent of a gender variant child, you are the captain of a sea-going ship. What is under your control? The seaworthiness of your ship, your preparedness for foul weather, the route you choose to get to port, the training of your crew, and your own training. It is your responsibility to negotiate whatever waters you meet on the way to port, but it is fantasy to assume that you can control those waters. As for blame, if you suddenly find yourself in a storm, are you more likely to get to port if you blame yourself for allowing the storm to happen? Of course not.

Let's say that you see another ship, headed to a different port, also caught in the storm. Does it make any sense to blame the captain of that ship for your predicament? Again, no.

Does it help to blame the storm? Cursing the rough sea wastes needed energy and distracts you from your responsibility: getting to port safely. You are much more likely to succeed if you simply accept the storm as a fact, the condition that you find yourself in, and rely upon your expertise to ride it out.

Will it help to ignore the storm the way that most of us ignore a pending confrontation, hoping that it will magically change course?

No, if you ignore the storm, it could broadside you, capsizing the ship. So, knowing that you can recover from the detour, you ride out the storm, allowing it to take you off course for a while.

Opal, one of the moms I interviewed, found herself in rough seas when her brother Lawson and sister-in-law, Ginny, refused to accept her trans son, Ira. Opal was particularly fond of Ginny, and the two families had been so close that they co-purchased a lakeshore home so that they could vacation together in the summer. When Ira came out to Opal, she spoke to Lawson and Ginny and sent them information prior to the family vacation. Despite that, once the families were together at the lake, Lawson and Ginny would not allow their eleven-year-old son to see Ira or even be in the same room with him. Needless to say, it was a difficult week.

Despite such thick tension, it is possible for Opal to confront the problem without alienating anyone. Since a three-way conversation would be far more complex and difficult to negotiate, she is more likely to succeed if she works with the less hostile person first, in this case Lawson. Before starting, she needs a plan that allows her to remain supportive of her brother even while she is confronting him about the problem. One workable plan for this situation can be broken down into six parts:[128]

1. **Recognize and state ownership of the apparent problem.** It's important for Opal to acknowledge that she is the one with the problem. It would, no doubt, be more comfortable for her to insist "It's *their* problem, not mine," but if she is honest with herself, she will recognize that she is very upset with situation. Although Lawson and Ginny may have their own problems, this is *her* problem, and if she wants it to be solved, she needs to take action. To own the problem, she starts with an *I* statement: *"I have a problem, and I need your help. I am upset by things as they are now. I feel abandoned, and Ira, Henry and I need the support of as many people as possible. I was hoping that I could count on you even though this is very difficult to understand and accept."*

2. **Describe the basis of the conflict in terms of behavior, consequences, and feelings**. It is important to include all three items: to describe what Lawson and Ginny have

done, what consequences that behavior has created and how those consequences make her feel. One possible way for Opal to express this is to say, *"We have always enjoyed our time together here—even aligning our vacations so that our families can be together—but keeping Ira and Gary apart is stressing us all out. I miss the warmth and sense of connection that we've always had. I don't want to lose that, but I feel us moving away from each other into isolation.*

3. **Avoid evaluating motives.** Opal needs to remember that she is focusing on *her* problem. Invariably, when we try to imagine the motive behind some else's behavior that bothers us, we fall back into fault-finding and blaming. Like all of us, Lawson and Ginny "have problems," no doubt a host of them, but if Opal allows herself to wonder, "What's their problem, anyway?" she will fall into a defensive mode of thought: "I know what they're up to—they have to protect their perfect kid from my pervert. So, they consider Ira a pervert and my support of him immoral!" She is better off to avoid creating any guesses about motives. Nobody wants to be told why they are doing anything, and any hint from Opal as to motives she might assume will close off the potential for reconciliation. Lawson might share his motives during the conversation. If he does, Opal will then be able to explore *his* motives rather than those that she had projected upon him.

4. **Be sure the other person understands your problem.** After speaking, Opal needs to listen openly to the response from Lawson to see if he has an accurate reading of her problem. If not, she should reword what she has to say then determine how her second attempt landed. If she can't get through, she can ask permission to table the discussion until she can find a way to make herself understood. Opal might say, *"This isn't working. I must be too upset to make myself clear right now. I need some time to figure out how to help you understand where I'm coming from. Let's put this off until this afternoon, okay?"*

5. **Think before you speak and be brief.** Opal can rehearse with a willing ally, perhaps Ira or Henry, to role-play the scene prior to taking on the confrontation. She needs to

be concise, because she wants to start a conversation, not deliver a lecture. Lawson will be engaged only if Opal offers an authentic invitation to him to help solve her problem. Allowing herself to "go on" will just open the door for saying things out of emotion rather than from her plan.

6. **Finish with a request that focuses on common ground.** This can be a challenge because when we find someone's behavior offensive, common ground can be difficult to uncover. What is the common ground in Opal's situation? One way to find it is to consider how you would finish this sentence: "We both have . . ." For example, *"We both have enjoyed our time together,"* or *"We both value the closeness and support of family."* Lawson may not understand what is happening with Ira, but Opal needs his help to get through this. Having established the common ground, she can now ask, *"I'd like to work with you to find a way that we can recapture that closeness."*

You may be saying to yourself, "That's all fine, but my situation isn't like that. It's not that I need to confront someone. My problem is that someone else is in my face and being very inappropriate." In that case, we can use a similar strategy that can help you address someone who is aggressively pressing a conflict.

The most egregious example of such behavior that I encountered in my interviews is the scene related by Viv about her daughter-in-law pounding on the bathroom door, assuming that Viv's trans son, Brent, was molesting his niece. An outsider might glibly say that Viv should just write the daughter-in-law off, but let's look at this from Viv's position. This is not just some woman who is out of control. It is your son's wife. You may want to write her off, but would you want to also write off your relationship with your son and your grandchildren?

Given the level of hostility that the daughter-in-law is exhibiting, this is not the moment for you to attempt a conversation that addresses the problem. You may have to wait for her to say or do something else hurtful but when she is not so emotional. Relax, she's bound to provide you with another opportunity. You probably won't have to wait long.

But where do you start? What can you do in this moment?

1. **Put up your shield**. Don't allow yourself to react.[129] You cannot control the situation or defuse tension if you cannot stay in control of yourself. The result of just letting yourself react would heighten tension further, which accomplishes nothing for anyone involved. If you can contain your anger enough to invent a zinger on the spot, you might feel momentary satisfaction that you managed to get one-up on your daughter-in-law, but you also undermine the warm, loving relationship that would be ideal. It may help if you visualize an invisible barrier that deflects the emotions and attitudes that are being hurled at you.

2. **Pay attention to nonverbal as well as verbal messages.** Your daughter-in-law is pounding on the door, not tapping. She's shouting, not whispering. She is offering plenty of evidence that she is out of control with anger and worry. It merely reinforces what she is feeling if you respond in kind. Take note of your own nonverbal cues: posture, eye contact, tone of voice. What you *do* is at least as important in this moment as what you *say*. If your goal is to defuse the situation, it won't work to stand in front of her, hands on hips and shout, "What the hell is wrong with you?" By contrast, you could just lean forward and offer an explanation, *"Hey, Brent went in there alone."* There is no guarantee that she will respond rationally, but at least you will not have added fuel to the flames.

3. **Respond empathically with genuine interest and concern.** This step is probably the most challenging part of the process, and it is probably not realistic to attempt it when tensions are running high. It is far easier to envision yourself being protected by an impenetrable bubble than to step out of your bubble and into the daughter-in-law's to see life from her perspective. What could you possibly say to her? Certainly she is showing no respect for Brent and a great deal of fear of him as well. The bottom line for her is her fear for her child—fear of predation. In a quieter moment you might say, *"I can understand your need to pro-*

tect your child. As a parent, I can see why you would be concerned. At first I couldn't accept it either, and I assumed that there had to be something seriously wrong with Brent."

4. **Paraphrase your understanding of the problem, and ask questions to clarify issues.** Once you have gotten to the point that you sense what may really be going on for her, you can venture a guess. *"It seems to me that you are absolutely committed to protecting your child, which I can understand. Every mother wants to be sure that her kid is safe. Is that what your concern is?"* If she says something as unfeeling as, "No, I don't see why you even let that deviate in the house," what do you say next? Don't *say* anything. Ask. One possible choice, *"Could you explain what you mean by deviate?"* This question moves you forward in that it engages her in helping you to define the problem.

   During this part of the process, you are exploring the behavior-consequences-feeling connection just as you would in step 2 of the previous strategy. For example, *Let me see if I get this right. By accepting him in my home, it puts you in contact with him, which you don't want. How does that make you feel?"* Rather than telling her how she feels, you are asking her to provide information, helping her to be part of the process. Explore what her concerns are fully. What does she assume might happen? Is safety of her child the only concern? Is she concerned that her child will be exposed to ideas that she finds objectionable?

5. **Seek common ground by finding some aspect of the complaint to agree with.** If you manage to focus on the problem rather than your response to the problem, you have a better chance of being able to see the situation from her perspective. In this case, you could say, *"I can agree with the need for safety and your willingness to take action even though others may not agree with you. I can understand your fear of her being exposed to ideas that you oppose, and I agree that we should work to avoid that."*

6. **Ask the person to suggest alternatives.** Now that you have demonstrated that you are listening to the other person and are working to address the underlying issues, you have gone a long way to diffuse the tension. You may find

that the suggestions made actually seem workable to you. If not, take the time to explain why. If, for example, she were to say, "Brent should not be allowed to be here," you can counter with this: *"Brent is my child, and his safety is important to me, so I can't abandon him, especially now when he is most vulnerable. But, how about if I come out to visit you next time, rather than your coming here."*

Don't expect the outcome to be ideal, but do be sure that it is something that you can accept at least in the short term. Ideally, Viv wants to have her family whole again rather than compartmentalized with Brent separated from his niece. It's perfectly fine to buy time by saying something like, *"Okay, I can accept that for now. But I want us to continue working on this together."* Remember to end by requesting a commitment to continuing the dialogue. It may take time for tensions to cool.

Of course, you are going to encounter, no doubt have already encountered, situations that are not a match for those discussed so far in this chapter. Working with your child and within your immediate family to maintain an open and supportive environment is one thing. Dealing with the responses that all of you receive from outside this inner circle is quite another. How do you and your family deal with unfeeling or pugnacious reactions of others? What do you say to a friend who tells you, "That's just sick!" First, it's useful to keep in mind that such a response is not actually directed at you or your child. It's directed at the experiences your friend has had and the assumptions that she has built around them. What you are hearing are the reactions to the meanings that your friend has created around sex and gender, and there is probably no other topic on which there are such deeply held assumptions and hang ups. It may be a neighbor or a school official—or it could be a total stranger who considers it his duty to put you in your place and let you know how disgusting it is for you to even allow your child to remain in your house or in your life.

So what do you do with these people?

First, consider how significant they are in your life. If this is a total stranger who you will never see again, it is probably not worth your trouble to become engaged or enraged. It may, however, be worthwhile to provide them with something to think about. Again, there is nothing to be gained in responding provocatively. Although it might feel gratifying to "put him in his place," it is also not likely to jog him toward a more open mind. I have spoken to many parents who say something like, "If they respond negatively, I just write them off." This attitude closes the door to moving the larger conversation forward. Yes, you may only be having a conversation with one person, but there are thousands of parents with gender-nonconforming people on the globe. Ask yourself, "How much progress would be made in our effort to move this conversation forward if everyone were to say what I just said?" In essence, we are working to bring gender nonconformity out of its global closet, and the more we invite people into the conversation, the more open that closet door swings. So it is in our best interests as parents of gender-nonconforming kids to approach others and respond to them openly and supportively. After all, support, not one-upmanship, is what will serve our children best. The following are possible responses in such a situation:

> "Given the suicide rate for gender-nonconforming people, I'm doing what I can to work on this with the hope that I won't end up attending my kid's funeral."
>
> "It's a difficult and touchy subject for many people, but my child is too important for me to back away from this."
>
> "This has been a difficult process, but it's opening me to see how sheltered and narrow-minded I have been in the past."

If, rather than being a stranger, the person you are speaking to is someone with whom you have an ongoing relationship, you can try one of the strategies outlined earlier in the chapter. If your effort fails, it's possible to explain what you are attempting to do. Simply say something like, "Look, my kid is important to me and needs my support, but you're important to me as well and I don't want to blow you off. This is what I'm trying to do, but I must have screwed it up because we're still not on the same page." Then show them the strategy that you are attempting from this book. Explain how it's supposed to work and ask them for support in making it work.

Finally, be patient with yourself. Don't expect to read an idea and then apply it flawlessly with your first attempt. It's like riding a bicycle—expect the first few trips to be a bit wobbly.

CHAPTER 6

How Green the Grass

IN STARTING THIS CHAPTER I am reminded of a scene in Murray Schisgal's 1967 play, *Luv.* While bemoaning his deprived childhood, Harry complains about his breakfast being nothing more than watered down milk. Milt replies, "Coffee grounds, that's what I got," so Harry asks, "With sugar?" Milt answers, "Not on your life. I ate it straight, like oatmeal."

Yes, misery loves company, and we seem to gain a bizarre gallows-humor satisfaction in proving *our* misery to be more profound than someone else's. In fact, I have played into this mindset myself at the several points in this book when I point to our culture's strait-jacketed response to gender nonconformity. I am not alone; plenty of people have written about how much more open and accepting other cultures are compared to the United States. From all the complaining, one might think that there is a multitude of cultures more accepting of transsexuality and gender nonconformity than ours. During research for this book, I have heard parents bemoan how slow the U.S. is to catch on and have read authors who refer to many other countries as having more open attitudes. These include Thailand, Belgium, England, India, New Guinea, Malaysia, the Dominican Republic, Myanmar, Venezuela, New Zealand, Ethiopia, South Africa, Ghana and several others. In particular, the Native American culture has been described by many researchers as exceptionally open toward trans people.

To be sure, our culture does not provide the ideal environment for gender-nonconforming people. If it did, there would be no need for this book and the host of other books written to help people sort out the tensions and anxieties that they face because of gender discrepancy. In an ideal environment, we wouldn't need to justify or explain our child's behavior or fear for our child's safety. We would have nothing to hide and no need to turn to professionals for help. We wouldn't have to worry that our child might be assaulted or even killed for being who s/he is. We wouldn't need to fight for our child's acceptance and well-being at school, and our children wouldn't be forced to accommodate the girl-or-boy straitjacket as they negotiate their way through childhood and adolescence to a stable identity.[130]

Even families who work to fight gender stereotypes and to create openness in the play and behavior of their children succumb to the dominant insistence that we separate the sexes. Consider this description of the problem:

> A boy is *never* taught that he is *supposed* to play house or dolls, the two activities that would prepare him to take a full role in his home, and the two activities that are expected of girls. Some boys are taught that they can do these roles if they want to, even though it is primarily girls who like to play house and dolls. This is a weak and confusing message. If the best we can do is to "permit" boys these activities, even in our most liberal, countercultural families, then the best they will ever be able to do as men is "help out."[131]

Such subconscious indoctrination clearly restricts what a child is "allowed" to imagine when considering what kind of human being s/he might become.

Kate Bornstein points out that there is significant variation among gender-nonconforming people, so much variation that their mere existence could challenge the widely held assumption that there are two and only two genders. She argues that the reason such a challenge has not materialized is because our culture mandates that a person must pass unconditionally as male or female. As a result, rather than feeling free to challenge this constricting norm, trans people feel compelled to fit into it. The ironic result is that transgender people "strive for recognition within their new gender, and thus succumb to the privileges and chains of their new gender."[132]

Bornstein's has a point. Despite limited exceptions in parts of some urban areas and on some college campuses, the assumption that there are two and only two genders rules supreme. We seldom if ever see people crossing the line—a man wearing makeup or a woman riding solo on a Harley. On a day-to-day basis, we don't run into people who are parked somewhere between male and female, so the resulting stereotypes are quite clearly defined for our children. Consequently, our culture trains its transgender children to see their own behaviors, identities and needs as deviant and plants in them a deep-rooted, destabilizing sense of guilt and shame, the result being that therapists often have to work hard to help them confront the transphobia at the base of their own self-loathing before they can make significant progress.[133] Furthermore, the sense of isolation is often reinforced by people we might assume would be more accepting. There is, for example, a history of feminists who have ostracized trans men for denying their inborn femininity and trans women for appropriating femininity in an effort to more fully impose their male dominance. This tension, which arose in the 1970s, has subsided, and I point it out here, not to pass judgment, but to emphasize the degree of isolation to which trans people have been subjected. In addition, it should be pointed out that butch lesbians have faced more than their share of discrimination as well. The entire debate is a further reflection of the problem we explored in chapter one: our temptation to box people in (or out).

Even more damaging, therapists themselves are not immune to this cultural bias. Based on an assumption that a particular patient is not likely to present an attractive appearance in the preferred gender and that all effort to live in the preferred gender role is useless, a therapist might deny diagnosis, disqualifying the potential candidate for hormones or surgery.[134]

Is it any wonder then that transgender people see themselves as somehow "less than," as perverse and unlovable? Our culture is inherently disorienting and demeaning to them because is forces them to live and grow up in an environment that deprives them of role models and allows little if any room for them to understand themselves in comparison to others. For example, I have heard Cadence speak several times about her long struggle to come to terms, literally, with who she was. She had no words that allowed her to explore who she might be. From early childhood, she wondered if there was anyone else like her, and, finding no evidence that there was, she operated on the assumption that she was a freak of nature. She knew that she was different, but with no language to describe that difference and having only the binary norm available, she had no means of defining herself in a meaningful way. She spent nearly two decades adrift and detached. She knew that the role her culture had boxed her into was a torturous fit, yet she saw no alternatives.

Given such profound isolation, parental assurances of unconditional love offer scant solace from the daily reminders that one is at best a grotesque caricature of a human being, a monster who transgresses sacred taboos. I can only imagine what my child might have been thinking: "You say that you love me no matter what, but you don't know who I am or what a freak I am!" Facing all the evidence that they are "messed up," our children are told by our culture that, without doubt, they are dirty and shameful.[135] It is disheartening to know that Cadence's experience is not an anomaly. Judging from the families that I have spoken to, this profound sense of isolation and alienation is essentially universal among gender-nonconforming people regardless of their age. With support, many move beyond the self-loathing that results and gain a sense of self-worth and dignity. Most of them, though, arrive at that destination only after a torturous emotional journey.

Even if we employ the help of a supportive therapist, the stigma remains. It is clear that there must be something significantly wrong. If not, why is there a pathological diagnosis for it? And even though we might claim to be open-minded about mental illness and perhaps accept that there is a certain cachet in seeing a therapist, there are certain diagnoses that still evoke a response beyond sympathy. Our culture sees depression as acceptable—everybody feels blue upon occasion, bi-polar disorder as unfortunate—poor confused thing can't figure out if he's flying high or bottoming out, and schizophrenia as frightening—imagine actually hearing voices. But gender identity disorder? That's out there, well past the edge of understandable—what, she thinks she's a guy? Beyond frightening, "trannies" are just weird and are widely considered to be perverse or at least very kinky.

So, now that I have again underscored our own culture's shortcomings regarding transgenderism, what are these other cultures that allegedly handle the issue more humanely? Many of the parents that I have spoken to believe that Asian cultures are more accepting, most often mentioning India and Thailand, and a good deal has been written about the flexible interpretation of gender in these cultures. The argument here is that ancient traditions in cultural mythology have created open acceptance of gender nonconformity. Let us look at these cultures to see how their treatment of gender nonconformity compares to ours.

India and Thailand

Serena Nanda, a professor of anthropology at John Jay College, has written extensively about the *hijra* tradition of India. The *hijra* occupy a position that does not equate exactly within our understanding of sexuality or gender. Born as men, they dress and act like women and are often castrated.[136] As followers of Bahuchara Mata, one of many mother goddesses, they perform specific ceremonial functions at the birth of male children and at marriages. Nanda sees the *hijra* identity as an outgrowth of the court eunuch that has a five-hundred-year tradition. Furthermore, the Hindu religion contains multiple deities that exhibit ambiguous or transformed sex and gender,[137] so gender transgression taps into an undercurrent of power and acceptance in the Indian culture that is very foreign to our understanding. It is estimated that there are as many as one million *hijras* in India. Nanda argues that criminalization and repression of the *hijra* arose during British occupation then carried over to the Indian government.[138]

The *hijras* are not, however fully recognized citizens, and they live separate from the rest of the culture. A young man who identifies as a *hijra* leaves his family to join the *hijra* community, and it is likely that he will end up resorting to begging and prostitution to survive. Furthermore, he will have extremely low social status and may be abused and beaten by the police.[139] Nanda presents the *hijras'* potent network of support as evidence that India offers widespread acceptance of gender nonconformity, but this view is not universally accepted, and the network is seen by others as an attempt to resist systemic exclusion of *hijras* from Indian culture.[140] Moreover there is no tradition in India that offers support or a social role for trans men.

Here in the U.S., Thai culture is also assumed to be open and accepting of gender nonconformity.[141] This widely held, romanticized notion seems to stem from two sources: media coverage of Thai *kathoey* (ladyboys) who work as popular entertainers and the large number of gender reassignment surgeries that are performed in Thailand.[142] Sam Winter, who teaches at the University of Hong Kong, has done extensive research on transgenderism in Asia, particularly in Thailand. His research indicates that the picture is not so rosy as we might like to assume. Transgender people are subjected to rejection and even violence at home, are ostracized by peers, and are coerced to conform to gender stereotypes by school administrators, the result being that many leave school early. Winter cites two reasons for this widespread rejection: human rights law in Asia lags behind that of the West, and, thanks in large part to the West's approach that pathologizes gender nonconformity, transgenderism is assumed to be a mental illness, which carries significant social stigma.

Although the *kathoey* have enjoyed sensationalist prominence, authorities have cracked down, making employment even more difficult to attain and discouraging media exposure. If they are outed while serving in the military, *kathoey* are discharged for "mental illness," which significantly hinders employment options after discharge.[143] Even those with college degrees have minimal chances of finding professional positions. They are excluded from employment in public service and are likely to end up in very low-end jobs. The lives of those without education or family support often mirror those of the *hijra* in India: living in the street, facing abuse from the police, and resorting to sex work to eke out sustenance. When their looks fade, even sex work is erased as an option. Very little is known about older *kathoey*, and it is possible that many of them find it too difficult to maintain their transgender lives and revert to male identity.[144]

Considering Asia more broadly, some nations prohibit cross dressing or homosexuality, and a trans woman who considers herself heterosexual can face prosecution for engaging in sex with a man. Despite the elevated recognition that Western media has given to trans identities in Asia, a study of over 800 college students, revealed transphobia to be as widespread in Asia as in the West.[145]

The Native American Two-Spirit Traditions

Here at home, ancient Native American culture is also heavily romanticized and it is widely assumed within the trans community to have provided an idyllic existence for its gender-nonconforming members. I have heard dozens of people claim that the two-spirit traditions of Native American nations have always bestowed positions of reverence and power upon transgender people. I write this section to put that assumption in perspective. A relatively new term, two-spirit, was coined at a 1990 conference of gay Native Americans in Winnipeg, Ontario, and originated not from the culture of the reservation but from urban gay Native Americans in reaction to *berdache,* the term used traditionally by Eurocentric researchers. *Berdache,* rooted in an Arabic term that signified a younger subservient male who was subjected to sodomy, is now considered by most Native American gays to be racist and demeaning. I use the term in the body of this book only because there is no equivalent noun available.

There is ample evidence that the vast majority of Native American tribes have traditionally recognized gender roles beyond male and female, and almost all tribes included *berdaches,* usually natal males who took on the dress and duties of women, including having sex with men. There is also clear, though less pervasive evidence of female *berdaches* sometimes referred to as "warrior women," who took on male roles and dress. The *berdache* would perform specific functions for the community, and those functions, though often similar, were not identical across tribes. Although the *berdache* role was usually assumed for life, arctic tribes may have exhibited more flexibility. An Inuit family, for example, that had only daughters could choose one or two of the younger daughters to be raised as male from infancy and taught to help the father with hunting and fishing. At puberty, they might maintain a male identity or might revert to female status.[146]

During the 1980s and early 1990s some anthropologists argued that there was a direct correlation between the *berdache* tradition and current-day gays and trans people, especially trans women. Several books and articles from that period claim that, far from being ridiculed and reviled, gender deviation was cherished and that two-spirit people wielded significant power. Emphasizing what they presented as openness and acceptance, researchers went so far as to argue that there was something close to gender parity within some Native American cultures with women and men sharing power and influence.[147] These claims have come under attack as simplistic and more hopeful than accurate. Among those who take exception to these depictions of the two-spirit tradition is Sue-Ellen Jacobs, who argues that after becoming aware of the influence and power of one uniquely prominent and charismatic *berdache*, researchers projected that same prominence to all two-spirit people.[148] Sabine Lang notes that many researchers interviewed other members of the community rather than the *berdache* and that it's likely that community members were feeding the researcher, who they knew to be a gay man, what they thought he wanted to hear.[149] Patrick Califia considers attempts to describe pre-European-invasion behavior among Native Americans as nothing more than speculation.[150] Finally, Richard Trexler argues that, despite revisionist attempts to sanitize the practice, evidence from historical research shows that the role of *berdache* was assigned to a child by tribal elders, not freely chosen by the child.[151] Trexler also argues that, as biological males, *berdaches* were physically more imposing than women and often assumed leadership roles among women, thus helping tribal elders to maintain male dominance. I offer one further slap at the romantic notion of Native American culture as bliss: Native American communities are just as likely to be as rabidly homo- and transphobic as any American community.[152]

In our effort to understand what is happening with our children and to legitimize their experience, it is comforting to believe that there are cultures that would cherish our children and to imagine connections to such cultures where they don't exist. Even though there may be correlations between two-spirit people and our trans children, those correlations should not be over-emphasized or oversimplified. Although there is some evidence that some tribes revered two-spirit members, others ridiculed them.[153] The Native American two-spirit tradition was multi-faceted and differed greatly from tribe to tribe. Although male and female two-spirits fulfilled roles that were different from those of men and women, the status, social roles, dress, and sexual activities of two-spirit people differed greatly among tribes. As discussed in chapter three, Sandra Bem suggests that there is value in sometimes looking *at* our filters rather than *through* them. If we do so we can guard against the tendency to project our assumptions and restrictions upon Native American cultures in an effort to find solace in a correlation that exists only in our desire to normalize what is going on with our children.

Traditional Native American understandings of gender and sexuality bear no comparison to those of Eurocentric cultures. Two-spirit members of most tribes were seen as third and fourth genders that were distinct from men and women, but traditional Native American cultures seemed to have drawn no distinction between heterosexuality and homosexuality. Their construction of gender was evidently more flexible, complex and nuanced than ours, and their construction of sexuality less burdened with anxiety and judgment. Having sex was simply having sex, regardless of the gender or the natal sex of the partner in the sex act, and the act was not charged with the social stigma and significance that today's American culture projects upon it. Let's isolate an example. The Navajo term for a *berdache* is *nadle* which translates roughly to "changing one" or "transforming one." So a man who had sex with a *nadle* was merely having sex with a *nadle*, and he would not consider the coupling to be a homosexual encounter—nor would others in his community. In fact, the concepts of homosexuality and heterosexuality would make no sense to him. If we were to say to him, "But you just had anal intercourse with another man," his response would be something like this: "That was a *nadle*, not a man. And your point is what?"[154]

That example illustrates the opaqueness of differing cultural perspectives. A social constructionist would explain the confusion this way. We learn how to be a human being by absorbing our culture's assumptions, and by the time we reach adolescence, through no choice of our own, we become the type of person our culture believes can exist. We speak its language and think its thoughts. Its reality has become our reality, "its impossibilities our impossibilities."[155] This creates a problem for us parents of a transgender child because our child has cast off our culture's rules and has become an impossibility. I have spoken to parents who had read enough to learn of the two-spirit tradition and they seemed to enjoy referring to their child as "our two-spirit child." None of them realized what an affront that description is to Native Americans. I have asked two-spirit people for their response to such a statement, and their reactions are quite consistent: they find it offensive. Gary Bowen, a self-described gay Native American cowboy, provides insight into this problem:

> There are many "magpies" who are drawn to latch onto the bright, shiny aspects of Native culture, who misappropriate Native culture, customs, and artifacts in the belief that they are "honoring" Native people by imitating them without understanding them. It is better for non-Native people to follow their own example by looking to

their own ancestors and reclaiming their own transgendered spirituality. European cultures from the Vikings to the Greeks had and honored transgendered people; even the Christian Church recognized saints that lived as members of the opposite sex and engaged in same-sex unions. No European culture lacks a transgendered tradition; white people need to reclaim their own sacred people instead of appropriating ours.[156]

The problem for us is that, never having been exposed to the history of our transgender ancestors, we don't know how to help our children put their experience into perspective, but it certainly does not help them to be given false or misleading information. We may eventually find better terms than trans child, transgender, or gender-nonconforming. Meanwhile, I prefer to remain mindful of the countless ways that we have already co-opted aspects of Native American culture in inaccurate, misinformed, and disrespectful ways. *Two-spirit* is a graceful and respectful term. I prefer that we not abuse it.

Europe

We have already seen in chapter five that attitudes during the Renaissance could be more open than we might expect, and there are a few limited accounts of gender flexibility. In her very popular book, *Transgender Warriors*, Leslie Feinberg argues that Joan of Arc was executed primarily because she insisted upon wearing men's clothing. Of course, that does not seem particularly flexible, but a key point that Feinberg makes in the book is that it was the church and the aristocracy that were troubled by Joan's recalcitrance. According the Feinberg, Joan was engaged in class warfare. Her army was pulled from the peasantry, which had no concerns about her wardrobe.[157] There are also accounts of women wearing men's garb, wielding men's weaponry, performing men's jobs and enjoying, at least to some extent, public recognition in the western Balkans since the first half of the 1800s and continuing until quite recently. Again, this practice was prevalent primarily among the rural/pastoral population.[158]

In recent history, the European nation most supportive of its trans citizens has been Sweden. There is evidence that the majority of Swedes not only support gender confirmation surgery but also the right of transsexuals to marry and to work with children,[159] The country passed a law in 1972 that made sex change legal, a law that has since become an international model. Germany, Italy, the Netherlands and Turkey have followed suit. In Austria the process is strictly administrative and does not involve the courts. In fact, all of the nations of the European Court of Human Rights confirm legal recognition of post-operative transsexuals.[160] Of course, only a small fraction of those who are gender-nonconforming have the desire and means to undergo surgery, which leaves the vast majority of trans people unprotected by such laws.

In the United Kingdom, the passage of Gender Recognition Act of 2004 gave transsexuals full legal rights, and, unlike other jurisdictions, the UK does not require a person to have undergone gender confirmation surgery to qualify. A trans person applies for recognition to a locally appointed Gender Recognition Panel that includes at least one lawyer and one health care professional or therapist. All members of the council understand transgender issues. This is a considerable advantage over the transgender person's plight on this side of the pond where the degree of legal protection depends upon which state or municipality one lives in.

Beyond the issue of full legal rights, reverse hormone therapy is covered by National Health care, which sounds quite supportive. There is, however, a problem: the treatment is not provided for anyone under sixteen. In other words, to have your child's hormone treatments covered, you must toe the line of National Health's protocol, which means you watch your child journey the wrong direction through puberty and endure the physical changes that s/he will later want to reverse surgically. If, like Jessica, the first mother that we encountered in chapter one, you choose to "leave the system," for example, by going to Belgium or the United States to help your child receive hormone blockers as she did, you are "out of the system" and receive no coverage whatever for issues related to gender nonconformity.

Led by Dr. Domenico Di Cegli, the position of the National Health Service is that adolescence is an important developmental period for the brain, and pubertal hormones may affect that development, affecting brain function and thus self concept. Di Cegli argues that to block these hormones in a child who identifies as transgender is to deny that child the possibility of being converted to "normalcy" by those coursing hormones. Evidence that this is likely to happen is lacking, and the preponderance of research suggests that thirteen-year-olds who identify as transgender are not "fixed" by undergoing unblocked puberty.[161]

Across the channel, Peggy Cohen-Kettenis, who is head of the Department of Medical Psychology and Medical Social Work at VU University Amsterdam, has been studying and treating transsexuals with a team of others for decades. This team takes a very different approach. After carefully screening teens who have presented symptoms of GID, they block hormones as early as age 13 and also provide cross-sex hormones as early as age 16. This has come to be called "the Dutch protocol," and some endocrinologists in the U.S. are putting it to use.

Although the Netherlands and Belgium may seem to be leading the way, they are not yet fully aligned with the most progressive set of guidelines for the treatment of gender nonconformity, the Yogyakarta Principles, which were established in November 2006 at a seminar held at Gadjah Mada University in Yogyakarta, Indonesia.[162] The principles were written by a team of internationally respected human rights experts, who called upon all nations to adopt the principles, which lay out specific protections in relation to sexual orientation and gender identity. Although there are twenty-nine separate principles in the document, the primary argument behind them can be summed up with the following excerpt:

> Everyone has the right to recognition everywhere as a person before the law. Persons of diverse sexual orientations and gender identities shall enjoy legal capacity in all aspects of life. Each person's self-defined sexual orientation and gender identity is integral to their personality and is one of the most basic aspects of self-determination, dignity and freedom. No one shall be forced to undergo medical procedures, including sex reassignment surgery, sterilization or hormonal therapy, as a requirement for legal recognition of their gender identity. No status, such as marriage or parenthood, may be invoked as such to prevent the legal recognition of a person's gender identity. No one shall be subjected to pressure to conceal, suppress or deny their sexual orientation or gender identity.

States shall:

1) Ensure that all persons are accorded legal capacity in civil matters, without discrimination on the basis of sexual orientation or gender identity, and the opportunity to exercise that capacity, including equal rights to conclude contracts, and to administer, own, acquire (including through inheritance), manage, enjoy and dispose of property;

2) Take all necessary legislative, administrative and other measures to fully respect and legally recognize each person's self-defined gender identity;

3) Take all necessary legislative, administrative and other measures to ensure that procedures exist whereby all State-issued identity papers which indicate a person's gender/sex—including birth certificates, passports, electoral records and other documents—reflect the person's profound self-defined gender identity;

4) Ensure that such procedures are efficient, fair and non-discriminatory, and respect the dignity and privacy of the person concerned;

5) Ensure that changes to identity documents will be recognized in all contexts where the identification or disaggregation of persons by gender is required by law or policy;

6) Undertake targeted programs to provide social support for all persons experiencing gender transitioning or reassignment.[163]

As we read through the above explanation, the opening statement is rather striking. In fact, you might have found yourself asking why it would be necessary for the Yogyakarta Principles to specify that surgery, sterilization, and hormone therapy not be required in order to be legally recognized. The answer? All three restrictions are standard requirements for gender reassignment surgery in Europe, even in those nations that are considered to be supportive. Transgender persons cannot have identity documents changed to affirm their new status unless these restrictions have been met. In essence, the state's insistence on all three steps reinforces the entrenched gender binary.

Once again, the trans person must jump into one of two boxes. A natal male who identifies as female but who prefers to avoid alteration of her body is forced to retain male identity documents. The option for her to park someplace in the middle of the gender continuum is available only if she is willing to become a non-person.[164] Furthermore, the surgery requirement presents an additional obstacle in that it assumes that transsexuals are MTFs since very few FTMs are willing to embrace the risks and complications inherent in phalloplasty. Did you notice one additional demeaning restriction in that opening paragraph? To have their identities recognized, trans people in Europe must be single. Marriages must be officially dissolved through divorce, annulment or automatic dissolution.[165]

Here in the U.S., we face a patchwork of legal policies, but our child's fate doesn't seem that daunting in comparison to the limitations that abound elsewhere. It's true that in some states, such as my home state of Ohio, your child's birth certificate cannot be altered regardless of circumstances. In contrast the process is quite simple in Minnesota. But changing a birth certificate is not always necessary. In New York, for example, an official name and gender change is relatively straightforward. Once the chosen name is legally established, documents such as a driver's license, social security card and passport can be updated accordingly.[166] Of course, it would be great if transgender rights were not dependent upon one's state of birth or residence, but there is at least some degree of flexibility. Although a progressive federal law is not likely to be a reality in the foreseeable future, there are pockets of acceptance, and we do have the sixteen states that recognize gender identity as legally protected.[167]

Even though the Yogyakarta Principles have engendered some positive responses which acknowledge them as a useful set of human rights guidelines, notably from the Netherlands, Canada, Uruguay, Brazil, and Argentina, the purpose of the principles is not to dictate laws to nations. Since their writing, the principles have been used as guidelines for Non-Government Organizations working around the globe, have been discussed at regional conferences on four continents and have been used as teaching tools in universities in the U.S., UK, China, Brazil, Argentina, and the Philippines.[168] It is unfortunate that so far U.S. public policy has ignored these principles, leaving it to academics to consider their value.

The DSM: Bible or Mere Cultural Artifact?

Up to this point, our discussion of cultural responses to gender nonconformity has ignored a key issue. As noted in the discussion about Thailand earlier in this chapter, the fact that the West considers gender nonconformity to be a psychological condition has global consequences, and there is an ongoing debate as to whether GID and GIDC should be included in the DSM. This debate does nothing to help beleaguered parents who are looking for clear answers that will help them to address their child's distress. When they first learn of the DSM and its diagnosis of GIDC, they may feel a sense of relief because now their child has an identifiable disorder that has a name and a nifty acronym. But upon further investigation, they find that the diagnosis provides little clarity because treatment for GIDC follows two conflicting paths. Along one path, we find parents working with the therapist to alter the child's behavior, the goal being to coach the child to fit into culturally defined norms. Along the other path, we find the parent-therapist team working to help the child explore feelings and behaviors and also working to make the environment more accepting, the goal being to reduce the amount of stress the child experiences.

To add to the confusion, the DSM is currently undergoing a major revision, and the debate of GID/GIDC is a prominent part of that revision. In essence, the participants in this debate are divided into two factions: one faction considers the DSM's approach to gender nonconformity to be a passage in psychology's bible that may need revision but primarily needs to be recertified; the other faction sees the DSM as a document that needs to reformed because it has been used to reinforce culturally defined assumptions about gender. Parents find themselves in the midst of a feud between the recertifiers and the reformers.[169]

The recertifiers tend to be conservatives. They accept the DSM as stemming from well established scientific principles, and they consider psychology to be an objective science that produces observations and diagnoses that are based on objective criteria. If you cannot measure something, it does not exist, and the DSM provides a reliable means of measurement. If a child matches enough of the symptoms described in the DSM, that child is diagnosed as having GIDC. Choosing not to follow the DSM or to question its validity as a diagnostic tool, amounts to heresy and is unethical. The therapist who does not follow the DSM strictly, is setting her/himself up as an independent agent and is choosing to ignore the vast body of work that peers have relied upon in the past. If all therapists were to operate in this fashion, the result would be chaos and the foundation of psychology as a viable discipline would be shaken. The most adamant recertifiers would argue that maverick therapists who treat the DSM as flawed are promoting illness rather than curing it.[170]

Recertifiers consider it their duty to help patients relieve emotional/psychological stress and to adapt to the expectations of society in order for them to live a well-adjusted life. They would argue that for adults the diagnosis provides relief by clearing the way for hormone therapy and surgery. The therapist functions as a gatekeeper for the patient, and the therapist's use of the GID diagnosis opens the door for the patient to receive much needed medical treatments. For a child, again the intention is to relieve stress, and therapy sessions focus on conditioning the child to adopt the behaviors associated with the child's natal sex. Kenneth Zucker, the most widely recognized of the recertifiers, conducts therapy that aims to reverse a child's cross-gender behavior for three reasons: (1) it reduces social ostracism, (2) the behavior may merely be a coping mechanism for separation anxiety, and (3) early intervention might reduce the chance of adult transsexualism.[171] Recertifiers believe that the therapist who fails to help the patient focus on adapting to societal norms is subjecting the patient to rejection, isolation and ridicule. The purpose of therapy is to help the patient to fit into the parameters that society considers to be normal. In other words: fix the patient.

In contrast to the recertifiers, we have the reformers, who tend to be liberals and progressives and who disagree with the above argument. Let's take a look first at their position on the DSM's approach to children. From the reformers' perspective, the assumptions of the recertifiers and the resulting treatments do nothing more than reinforce cultural stereotypes around gender by training young boys to be tough and aggressive and young girls to be passive and compliant. What is worse, by reinforcing these stereotypes, the APA is putting its stamp upon these behaviors as officially recognized, thus appropriate and "normal." Reformers point out that the DSM itself is based on timeworn stereotypes. In fact, the current DSM includes the following criteria for GIDC which openly acknowledge dependence on stereotypes: "in boys, preference for cross-dressing or simulating female attire; in girls, insistence on wearing only stereotypical masculine clothing," and "intense desire to participate in the stereotypical games and pastimes of the other sex." Since the clothing, games and pastimes are not specified, it is left to the individual therapist to determine what they might be, but it's not hard to imagine that for boys this list includes briefs or boxers, jeans and t-shirts for clothing. As for behaviors, a boy should enjoy rough-and-tumble play, ball play, and team sports—in essence: aggressive, physical activities. For girls the list of clothing would include panties, skirts and dresses, and behaviors would include doll play, dress up and house keeping—in essence: passive, sedentary activities.

Reformers also see gender bias in the DSM. Since our culture sees boys as boisterous, we assume that their behavior needs more supervision than that of girls. The language of the DSM criteria mirrors that assumption with its focus on reining in the behavior of boys, who need only to *prefer* to wear feminine attire to match the diagnosis. To fit the DSM criteria, a girl must *insist* upon male attire. Of course, the result is that far more boys than girls are then diagnosed. Adding to the fire, the APA appointed Kenneth Zucker to chair the committee that is working to revise GID and GIDC for DSM-V, which suggests that no wholesale alterations will be forthcoming. The current proposed revisions have replaced *stereotypical* with *typical* and *insistence* with *preference*. The revisions do not, however, address what reformers consider to be flawed assumptions in the DSM: (1) behaviors are separated into recognizable and dichotomous male and female patterns; (2) failure to follow those patterns constitutes pathology.[172] For reformers, retention of GIDC will encourage therapists to reinforce flawed stereotypes. Here is a typical reformer interpretation:

> [GIDC] appears to many [to be] an instrument of social control whereby children and youth who demonstrate variability in gender are pathologized and "treated" to conform to society's expectations for gender. A less controversial approach, respectful of increasing gender freedom in our culture and sympathetic to a child's struggle with gender, would be more humane. Ultimately, in the absence of strong research justifying GID in children and adolescents, and in the face of growing opposition,

clinicians and researchers might just have to rely on humanistic and moral judgments as how to best help gender nonconforming children and adolescents.[173]

So, rather than treating the DSM as if it is based solely on verifiable objective evidence, reformers accept the impact of culture and societal pressures on the DSM. They argue that the manual, which has adapted to social changes in the past, should not resist doing so now and that GID/GIDC should be removed from the DSM-V because gender identity and expression are being redefined and are becoming far more varied than in the past. This part of their argument relates to treatment of adults as well as children.

Many reformers believe that adult GID is being used to force trans adults to conform to stereotypes. A trans person gains access to medical treatment only after a therapist confirms pathology, and it is assumed that, after transition, the patient will live life in stealth mode, calling as little attention to her/his gender as possible. We have made progress since the middle of the twentieth century when patients had to swear to live a "straight" life after transition in order to gain access to medical treatment. The problem here is that, like the general population, most trans people are quite well adjusted and well functioning and do not consider themselves to be "disordered." They hold jobs, raise children, and serve their communities. In short, they do everything that you and I do. The difference is that they do one more thing: stay in the closet. They work consciously to fit into the new box that they are placed in by their transition.

Some reformers further emphasize the culture-bound and politicized nature of the DSM by pointing out its history with homosexuality, which was listed as a disorder in DSM-I in 1952, but within a space of three years in the early 1970s the entry on homosexuality was revised then removed when the APA clearly yielded to pressure from gay rights advocates.[174] There are also reformers who argue that it is more than just coincidence that GID entered as a new disorder in the DSM after homosexuality was deleted. Recertifiers point out that homosexuality was removed from the DSM seven years before GID was added and that there was no hidden agenda to replace homosexuality with GID.[175]

The most visible of the recertifiers has been Robert Spitzer, who retired in 2010 from Columbia University and who chaired the task force that eliminated homosexuality from the DSM in 1973. Spitzer insists that the DSM is based on solid scientific foundations and is not influenced by culture or social pressures. Despite that, he has been quoted as saying that politically sensitive disorders will stay in DSM-V because their removal would create a "public relations disaster for psychiatry."[176] He has not explained how that statement squares with his past insistence that culture does not influence psychiatry.

Given the vehemence of the two camps, the debate is not likely to end soon. Despite that, there are plenty of therapists who are fully aware of the nuances of this debate and realize that, regardless of the debate and the current status of GID as a diagnosis, their job is to find ways to support their patients and the families of those patients to alleviate suffering. Therapists who understand the benefits and limitations of the DSM are in a position to use their expertise to the patient's and the family's advantage. Hormone therapy and surgery create results that are irreversible, and such options need to be carefully weighed. The decisions made regarding gender transition, whether for a young child or an adult, have a profound impact for the patient and the family, so these decisions need to be made with an awareness and understanding of the many burdens and issues that accompany the process.

It's logical that parents who face this dilemma want to know the details, but it's not necessary or even possible for us understand all the details. We need enough information to have an understanding of what we and our families face and enough support to know that we are not operating in a vacuum. Luckily there are psychotherapists, endocrinologists, and surgeons who are willing to provide that information and support. With their help and enough patience and resolve, we can find our way through the maze that confronts us.

ENDNOTES

1. Burke 1996, 57.
2. Burke 1996, 196–7.
3. PFLAG (Parents, Families and Friends of Lesbians and Gays) is a national support and advocacy organization.
4. In the United Kingdom, gender identity disorder is treated through the National Health Service.
5. This is the first use of the "trans daughter" or "trans son" in the book. The respectful and empathic way to refer to a trans person is by acknowledging his or her sense of self. So I refer to Cadence as my trans daughter or a trans woman throughout. To call her my trans son or a trans man would be to assert that Cadence is not who she says she is and suggests that she does not know herself. The issue of language is fully examined in chapter three which deals with terminology.
6. While quoting herself in this manner, the mom who spoke these words revealed that she had grown to internalize the profound need that her child was asserting through transition. By the time that I interviewed her, she clearly understood how clueless her earlier responses had been and laughed aloud at her prior naiveté. Although we often gain a sense of levity about our struggles only in hindsight, we still benefit from the release that the levity provides.
7. Zucker and Bradley 1995, 223–6.
8. Previously referred to as hermaphroditism, which is now considered a slur. The extended list of terms in chapter three offers more detail.
9. Very few people know that the colors most associated with gender are themselves transgender. They switched genders in the 1920s. Prior to that, pink was considered the color for boys and blue the color for girls. In fact, a 1918 merchandising magazine

129

asserted that, because it was the more "decided and stronger" color, pink was appropriate for boys; whereas blue, being "delicate and dainty," thus "prettier," was the color for girls (Chiu, Gervan, et al. 2006, 385).

10. (Feinberg 1998, 27) Feinberg's comment was actually about coming out to a spouse, but it is not a stretch to compare that situation to coming out to a parent or a close friend or relative.

11. APA Task Force on Gender Identity and Gender Variance 2008 Nemoto, Operario, et al. 2004; Xavier JM, Bobbin M, et al. 2005. One additional point to consider is that, at the moment of coming out, gender-nonconforming people are particularly vulnerable, fearing isolation and feeling stigmatized (Bockting and Coleman 2007, 189–90).

12. You may also find it helpful to write about what you are experiencing and how you feel about it. James Pennebaker, the chair of psychology at the University of Texas at Austin, has researched the benefits of writing about trauma extensively. His research shows that people who write regularly about the facts of what is happening and about their emotions related to events enjoy better overall physical and psychological health (Pennebaker 1990, 34–40).

13. Hyman 2008, 11.

14. Kelly, Klusas, et al. 2001, 664.

15. Williams and Dolnik 2001, 214–16. Although Williams and Dolnik's research is based on the behavior of defense lawyers in a courtroom, it suggests that "stealing thunder" is likely to work if you are concerned that the person whose thunder you are stealing is likely to present your information in a negative light. Williams and Dolnik's research shows that lawyers universally agree that stealing thunder is so effective, that they never consider passing up a chance to use it.

16. Kelly 1999, 107.

17. Rodriguez and Kelly 2006, 1043.

18. The states that have employment and housing laws that specifically list gender identity as protected are California, Colorado, Connecticut, Hawaii, Illinois, Iowa, Maine, Massachusetts, Minnesota, Nevada, New Jersey, New Mexico, Oregon, Rhode Island, Vermont and Washington. As for hate crime laws that protect gender identity, unfortunately the list is shorter: California, Colorado,

Connecticut, District of Columbia, Hawaii, Maryland, Minnesota, Missouri, New Jersey, New Mexico, Oregon, Vermont and Washington. There also 143 municipalities or counties that that offer protection against discrimination. Sources: http://www.hrc.org and http://www.transgenderlaw. org. Luckily, the list continues to grow.

19. I base the strategies suggested here on Lev 2004, 285 and Israel and Tarver 1997, 52.

20. Lev 2004, 245.

21. Bockting and Coleman 2007, 190.

22. Stuart 1991, 102.

23. Unless you live in one of the states listed before or in a municipality that protects gender identity and expression, your daughter may have no recourse even if her boss were to fire her on the spot and say something as crass as, "We don't need perverts like you working here."

24. My discussion here is drawn in part from Lev 2004, 70–85.

25. I use *natal* (birth) sex and purposely avoid *biological* sex throughout this discussion because the use of *biological* would suggest that the sex announced at birth is somehow a factual result of scientific investigation, which is not the case.

26. Fausto-Sterling 2000, 51–4

27. http://www.isna.org.

28. Despite this general tendency, girls are boxed in as well. A woman who loves her Harley is assumed to be a butch lesbian and gets more than her share of scowls, head shakes and catcalls.

29. Unlike all the terms under discussion in this portion of the chapter, which have been explored by multiple researchers and theorists, my reading of the literature suggests that gender attribution is the product of one person, Kate Bornstein. She likens our tendency to make this judgment automatically to barreling along a crowded highway in a sixteen wheeler without paying attention to where we are going (Bornstein 1994, 26).

30. Diamond has argued for use of both these terms as well as *ambiphilia* instead of bisexualism (Diamond 2006, 590).

31. Terms for sexual orientation can be confusing during research. Many academic journal articles continue to use the traditional definitions, which date back to the nineteenth century and describe sexual orientation in relation to natal sex. As a result

"male transsexual" would refer to a trans woman as defined in this book and by the trans community. If that "male transsexual" is attracted to women, the researcher will refer to "him" as heterosexual—further evidence that *gynophilic* would be more accurate and understandable.

32. Bem's scale, the BSRI (Bem Sex Role Inventory) has come under attack for its use of stereotypical definitions of gender roles. To establish cultural norms, she isolated the most typical responses of males and females to the inventory in the 1970s and used the most prevalent traits to establish her scale. Her purpose was to uncover those people who were "highly motivated to keep both their self-concept and their behavior consistent with the cultural standards of gender appropriateness (the conventionally sex-typed group) and those for whom the cultural standards of gender appropriateness are not particularly important to either their self-concept or their behavior (the androgynous group)" (Bem 1993, 120). Later explorations that followed Bem have provided some interesting results. One notable example indicates that the personal aspirations of transsexuals are not restricted by either their birth gender or chosen gender (Winter and Udomsak 2002).

33. A bit more on this term from http://kinseyconfidential.org/transgender-genderqueer-cisgender-terms: "*Cisgender* refers to people whose sex and gender are congruent by predominant cultural standards: women who have female bodies, men who have male bodies. This term was created to challenge, as many transgender people have argued, the privileging of such people in the term *gender* relative to the term *transgender*. For example, in referring to *trans men* (female-to-male transgender men) and *men* (cismen), it may seem that transgender men are always a special type of 'man,' while men are, without question, 'real men.'"

34. The APA Council of Representatives passed this resolution in 1997 and reinforced its position twelve years later in APA Task Force on Appropriate Therapeutic Responses to Sexual Orientation 2009. NARTH and other anti-gay organizations continue to support the practice.

35. This is a very contentious issue, and Ken Zucker is widely reviled in the trans community. The parents that I interviewed

who know of Zucker's treatment protocol consider it to be abusive. For his part, Zucker considers it worthwhile to help a child feel more comfortable with her/his assigned gender, which also assures that the child is less likely to be the victim of bullying and ostracism. He works with parents to condition the child to abandon cross-sex behaviors. Zucker sometimes does damage to his cause, for example pointing out that he finds that "educated" parents are not receptive and complaining that, according to social constructionists "one can never be the architect of one's own misery" (Zucker and Bradley 1995, 55).

36. As with *butch*, this term can be used as an adjective. It is difficult to pin down a precise explanation of the butch/femme phenomenon without going to some length. Although both terms have come to be used more broadly in some circles, femme and butch lesbians use both terms to define choices in clothing, body language and sexual behaviors. In many ways they have been marginalized as much as trans people. To gain a better understanding, read Leslie Feinberg's novel, *Stone Butch Blues.*

37. Gender-nonconforming people are not necessarily uncomfortable. It is quite possible for someone to be born as one sex, identify as the other sex and be comfortable with that discrepancy.

38. Bullough and Bullough 1993, 269. Henry Rubin argues that it was Benjamin who differentiated sex and gender (Rubin 2003, 33–34). Some conservative psychologists, most prominently Paul McHugh, refuse to accept any cultural impact on our understanding of gender. McHugh took over at Johns Hopkins, closing down the clinic and forcing Money out. He was quite influential during a conservative backlash in the 1970s, and he still scoffs at the idea of gender being separate from sexuality, essentially refusing to accept *gender* as a viable word in the discussion of sex roles (McHugh 2004, 38). He would dismiss the first several pages of this chapter as utter nonsense.

39. Bullough and Bullough 1993, 271.

40. Colopinto (2000) demonized Money, perhaps rightfully so, for his early approach to the treatment of children. Colopinto's book explores Money's most infamous case, that of David Reimer, which ended with Reimer's suicide at the age of 38.

41. Winter 2007. I offer a more thorough examination of this debate in chapter six.

42. World Professional Association for Transgender Health 2011, 21.

43. World Professional Association for Transgender Health 2011.

44. Granted, Halberstam is still within an academic community, but I have met several older people who refuse to be trapped in a single gender. Yes, they are rare, but they do exist.

45. I make this point not to suggest that trans men face no discrimination but to emphasize the dilemma faced by a trans woman.

46. Wallien and Cohen-Kettenis 2008, 1416.

47. Green 1987, 318. Although Green's methodology for determining adult gender identity outcome is a bit murky, he concluded that only one of the 44 boys ended up transsexual (see Zucker 1990, 16). It is difficult to use Green's work to draw any conclusions about persistence of trans gender identity because he did not distinguish gender identity or gender expression from sexuality. The focus of his study was on homosexuality, not gender identity.

48. Wallien and Cohen-Kettenis 2008, 1420.

49. Wallien and Cohen-Kettenis 2008, 1420. This study was based on a total of 77 children.

50. Zucker 2008, 1362.

51. Menvielle 1998, 243.

52. Five years may seem an incredibly young age for such a decision. Keep in mind, however, that the decision is not permanent. Although the child may stick with the transition, it is also possible to revert back. In addition, the transition is made only after careful consideration of all options by the parents, the child's pediatrician, the psychotherapist, and school personnel. The vast majority of parents that I have interviewed indicate that classmates adapt readily to the transition—often far more readily than adults.

53. Given the level of emotion on both sides of this debate, this series of questions with no attempt to answer them will, no doubt, raise some hackles. I have chosen to put my opinion in a note rather than in the body of the chapter. Of course the slant of the rest of this book probably makes that opinion obvious. As parents, Karen and I don't feel that we have ever had a right to determine an outcome for either of our children,

whether it be gender identity and expression or choice of voca-tion. Of course, we want a happy outcome for our children, but that happiness should be defined by them, not us. So, we clearly side with working *with* the child to find what way the journey will turn rather than working *on* the child to force a stereotyped outcome.

54. APA Task Force on Gender Identity and Gender Variance 2008, 30.

55. Winter and Udomsak 2002.

56. http://ai.eecs.umich.edu/people/conway/TS/TSprevalence.html.

57. Horton 2008.

58. Motmans 2010, 45.

59. Zucker and Bradley 1995, 31.

60. Citing Zucker and Bradley's estimate, Phyllis Burke argues that GIDC is clearly not rare (Burke 1996, 66).

61. Brill and Pepper 2008, 207.

62. Research by others and interviews with parents indicate that a father is likely to feel more confronted than a mother by a son who is gender-nonconforming.

63. The loss of custody may seem farfetched, but there are parents who have lost custody—including visitation rights—not only of the trans child, but of all their children.

64. Slow progress is being made with pressure building on insur-ance companies to offer more coverage. The American Medical Association House of Delegates composed a resolution in June 2007 requesting that insurance providers cover the medical needs of transgender persons. The American Psychological Association may soon be following suit: an APA task force on gender identity and gender variance published a report in December 2008 that requested that the APA adopt the same policy.

65. McHugh 2004, 38. McHugh is a particularly rabid right-wing critic of Spack and considers conversion therapy the only ethi-cal treatment for gender nonconformity. Spack has faced a sig-nificant amount of criticism on this issue from right-leaning Christian groups. He has been tagged as demonic by MassRe-sistance and barbaric by Americans for Truth about Homosex-uality. Equally vitriolic rhetoric has been used by trans-activist groups to describe Kenneth Zucker.

66. Spiegel 2008. In the U.K. all medical expenses are covered so long as the family adheres to the standards of care laid out by the Royal College of Psychiatrists that forbids any hormonal intervention, including hormone blockers, until age 16.
67. De Sutter, Kira, Verschoor, et al. 2002. Insurance would not cover the cost of preserving the sperm, adding another financial burden to the process.
68. De Sutter, Kira, et al. 2002.
69. Spiegel 2008.
70. Of course, every surgical procedure carries some risks of side effects. If no side effects are listed for a particular procedure, risks are considered to be minimal.
71. Willis 2005, 153.
72. Schaefer and Wheeler 2004, 123, note that some parents "are relieved to learn about the possibility of prenatal influence on gender conditions so they need not feel guilty for their child's rare and misunderstood dilemma."
73. A child can be invisibly gay, but that option does not exist for a trans child. See Schaefer and Wheeler 2004, 123.
74. Ladd-Taylor and Umansky 1998, 7–11. Ladd-Taylor and Umasky's reading of history is, of course, feminist in slant, but they provide a compelling explanation of the development of Momism.
75. You may have noticed that I have not mentioned girls. Since he saw the future as being defined by men, Wylie, was unlikely to consider girls important enough to be of concern to him or to the country's well-being.
76. Wylie 1942, 196–203. I do not pretend that my attempt at a brief history of Momism is complete. My intention is to highlight key factors in its development.
77. Much of what I offer here is indebted to Terry 1998, 176–83 which examines Strecker's political agenda from a feminist position.
78. Dallas Denny, a trans woman, provides some perspective on Benjamin's assumptions, explaining that in the 1990s transgender activists worked to set the record straight. Denny refers to Benjamin's model as the *transsexual* model and the newer model as the *transgender* model that enhanced "awareness among researchers and clinicians that genital sex reassignment surgery (SRS) is not uniformly desired or sought by all persons who

dress and behave as members of the other sex on a full-time basis" (Denny 2004, 26).

79. At the university clinics in the 1970s, doctors performed surgery only if they felt that the post-op patient would blend into society effectively enough to reflect well upon the institution. See Meyerowitz 2002, 226.

80. To Money's credit, he later revised this simplistic thinking on gender, acknowledging that the process of gender identity and expression was far more complicated than he had originally claimed. Unfortunately, his early approach has been widely accepted and followed without question for decades.

81. Stoller 1985, 29–56.

82. Green 1974, 57.

83. Green 1974, 41.

84. Yes, Mom again! See Green 1974, 211–13.

85. Lothstein 1983, 10.

86. Lothstein 1979, 221–2.

87. Rekers and Kilgus 1995, 264.

88. Rekers 1995, 284. Rekers is no longer a member of the APA because of his continued endorsement of reparative therapy for homosexuals. In 2008, he provided paid testimony in support of Florida's ban of adoption by gays.

89. Coates and Person 1985.

90. Zucker and Bradley 1995, 258–9.

91. Ladd-Taylor and Umansky 1998, 135. This book also examines how the advent of professional social work in the 1920s helped to establish the "case" against mothers. The staff of day nurseries cared for children of mothers who had to work. It was assumed that, unlike the mothers who could afford to stay at home, these financially disadvantaged mothers needed to be trained to provide adequate homes for their children.

92. Fausto-Sterling 2000, 36.

93. Mead 1935.

94. Hubbard 1990, 137.

95. Goffman 1977, 302.

96. Diamond might well consider this statement an over-simplification. He has argued from his earliest writings that the development of gender identity is the result of a complex intermingling of nature and nurture.

97. Hubbard 1990, 139.
98. Anne Fausto-Sterling wades through a detailed history of how hormones became gendered. See *Sexing the Body*, pp. 146-94. She charts out the chronology of events on pages 152-3.
99. Fausto-Sterling 2000, 178–79.
100. Fausto-Sterling 2000, 224.
101. For example, Swaab 2004, 307–8, cited several studies that support the influence of *in-utero* hormones, but the APA Task Force on Gender Identity and Gender Variance reported in 2008 that prenatal hormones do not influence gender identity. In 2010 Veale, Clarke, et al. 2010, concluded that they *may* do so.
102. de Lacoste-Utamsing and Holloway 1982, 1432. Notice that the authors are being doubly cautious, stating that *if* there are gender differences in brain functions, their findings *could* be related to those differences.
103. Fausto-Sterling 2000, 119.
104. Kruijver F.P., Zhou J.N. Pool C.W., et al. 2000, 2041. Again, the researchers do not publish any absolute claims. Their research shows that the central subdivision of the bed nucleus of the stria terminalis (BSTc) is larger in men than in women, including trans women. They caution that the number of specimens examined is small (7 brains of trans women).
105. Burke 1996, 189.
106. For example, in preparing a brain for inspection, the tissue first has to be pickled, and it is impossible to be certain of the degree to which the pickling process alters the tissue. MRIs have been used, but their images, though improving, are far less precise than microscopic examinations (Fausto-Sterling 2000, 124–5). To my knowledge there have been no studies using blood flow or electrical impulses to examine brain function that relates to gender nonconformity.
107. The debate is most hotly contested over the treatment of children. As discussed in chapter three, Kenneth Zucker and Norman Spack have both been accused of abuse.
108. For example Fausto-Sterling 2000, Lippa 2005, McLafferty 2006, Rutter 2006,, and Stotz 2008.
109. McLafferty 2006, 177, provides a nuanced critique of the nature-nurture paradigm, arguing that it assumes *exclusivity*

(only genes and culture create who we are—there are no other variables), *universality* (the nature-nurture paradigm explains every possible human trait), and *complementarity* (the more nature explains a trait, the less nurture. In other words, nature + nurture = one. Always.)

110. Fausto-Sterling 2000, 237, writes: "In short, DNA or genes don't make gene products. Complex cells do. Put pure DNA in a test tube and it will sit there, inert, pretty much forever. Put DNA in a cell and it may do any number of things, depending in large part on the present and recent past histories of the cell in question. In other words, a gene's actions, or lack thereof, depend on the microcosm in which it finds itself. New work, suggesting that as many as 8,000 genes can be expressed in a developmentally stimulated cell, shows just how complex that microcosm can be."

111. Fausto-Sterling 2000, 26.

112. Hubbard 1990, 138.

113. Lewontin is well-known as a leftist who is concerned that interest in the Human Genome Project and genetic determinism might be used to oppress people who are considered to be inferior.

114. There are many who have presented arguments against Galton's assumptions. Consider these observations: "Ask not what's inside the genes you inherited, but what the genes you inherited are inside of" (West and King 1987, 552); "The more we lift the lid on the human genome, the more vulnerable to experience genes appear to be" (Ridley 2003, 552); and "Those different dichotomies, such as innate–acquired, inherited–learned, gene–environment, biology–culture, and nature–nurture, are not just inappropriate labels in themselves but they do not map neatly onto each other: genes do not equal innate, biology, or nature, and neither does the environment stand for acquired, culture, or nurture" (Stotz 2008, 360).

115. Bockting and Coleman (2007) provide a discussion of several models, many of which can provide insight into the experience of any type of gender nonconformity, not just transsexualism. Also, Devor (2004) offers a 14-stage model for FTMs, which is available online at http://web.uvic.ca/~ahdevor/14Stages BLOCK.pdf.

116. Emerson and Rosenfeld (1996) seem to have based their observations on the more traditional model of a transgender adult child who is living separately from the family.

117. Ellis and Eriksen (2002) did not label their stages, so I have created labels for the sake of comparison.

118. Ellis and Eriksen 2002, 295.

119. For a more thorough discussion, see Ellis and Eriksen 2002, 295-7.

120. Lev and Alie, 58-59.

121. I have not been able to locate the original source of this approach, but there are several discussions available that explore this tactic. Just type "agreeing with the critic" into a web browser.

122. Gibb 1961. Gibb's explanation of communication climates is one of the most widely cited theories in interpersonal communication. Those who have written about this approach to communication climate often discuss it at more length than Gibb did.

123. Gibb's objection to strategy should not be confused with our chapter-two exploration of the planning that you complete before coming out to people. In that chapter, we examined how you prepare for a critical conversation. Once that conversation is started, it must be totally spontaneous. If not, there is no way that you can respond effectively to the issues that arise.

124. My discussion of "I" statements is based on Kubany, Richard, Bauer, et al. 1992.

125. This discussion and the graph are based on Thomas 1976.

126. James Pennebaker notes that at least one third of college students who seek therapy complain about their relationship with their parents and the majority of these students feel judged by their parents. Many of them choose to detach themselves from their parents (Pennebaker 1990, 121).

127. Fisher and Ury 1983.

128. Verderber and Verderber 2001, 325–33. The Verderbers created both of these six-part models by comingling suggestions from several sources. I have adapted their strategy slightly here.

129. The first habit in Stephen R. Covey's *The Seven Habits of Highly Effective People*, is proactivity, which he contrasts with reactivity. The reactive person allows her/his emotional

response to a situation to dictate behavior. The proactive person, however, bases behavior on values. If you value a loving relationship, you find behavior that reflects and furthers that value. As with all the strategies in this chapter, understanding how proactivity works is far easier than putting it to use.

130. Barrie Thorne has studied school climate closely and offers a compelling analysis of the troubled waters that gender-nonconforming children must wade through, noting that even the fiction that explores the experiences of tomboys and sissies is of little help. In fiction, sissies are portrayed as loners with no close friends—not even girls—who finally win due to a hidden or previously unrecognized male trait. In contrast, the tomboys of fiction get to have friends but eventually acquiesce, accepting the limitations dictated by society (Thorne 118–19).

131. Burke 133.

132. Bornstein 127.

133. For discussion of this issue see MacKenzie 45 and Bockting, et al. 196.

134. Judith Butler presents this argument (pp.9-10), and offers a nuanced examination of the complexities that confront gender-nonconforming people and their therapists in our culture.

135. Bem (332) makes a compelling argument that our culture equates being transgender with being dirt. In essence anything (or anyone) that transgresses a culture's "cherished classifications," for example, the classifications that we assume regarding gender/sex/desire, threatens the fabric of that culture and is considered dirt, becoming intolerable—not to be acknowledged or even mentioned. In order to retain moral balance, the dirt must be swept under the rug (or closeted). This point was driven home for Karen and me years ago when we had Cadence's first therapy group over for a meal. They were astounded that we invited them into our home because every one of them had been totally estranged from family upon coming out.

136. A few *hijras* are born female but are infertile (Nanda 383).

137. Nanda 375–77.

138. Nanda 380.

139. *Ravaging the Vulnerable: Abuses Against Persons of High Risk of IIIV Infection in Bangladesh* 40.

140. Hall 431.

141. Ironically, stereotypes are as shallow and sensationalized in Thailand as they are here in the U.S. Equally ironic, *Kathoeys* often assume that attitudes in the U.S. are extremely liberal and accepting of gender nonconformity (Costa, et al. 7).

142. Although in the West, the term *kathoey* is accepted in the narrow sense of "ladyboy," in Thailand it is used as an umbrella term for any deviation from heterosexuality or traditional male gender expression. In general, Thais, like Americans, do not separate gender from sexuality, so a Thai would use *kathoey* to refer to a gay man, a drag queen, a transsexual or a cross dresser (Costa, et al. 17–19).

143. Winter.

144. Winter and Udomsak.

145. This finding is based on research done by Winter and others in 2007 in seven countries: China, Malaysia, Singapore, Thailand, the Philippines, the United Kingdom and the United States. The study showed that across all countries students generally believe that trans people are mentally ill and that trans women are sexual deviants who are not real women. They also indicated that they would avoid contact with trans women, even within family (Winter).

146. Trexler (619-20) notes that children were chosen for gender reassignment when the family was "far enough along in a marriage where the absence of the desired sexed child gave concern to the parents." In the arctic tribes, most of the *berdaches* have been natal females, but a family lacking girls might also raise one or two of the younger sons as female to assure that the mother had adequate help to fulfill her role. Regarding the possible reversion to natal sex identity at puberty, Trexler points out that this may not have been allowed until tribes felt constrained by the expectations of newly arrived European missionaries.

147. See Roscoe, Changing Ones 97–8. Roscoe did not pretend that *berdaches* lived idyllic lives, and in separate writing he argued that gender nonconformity was the least important factor in defining the role of a *berdache* (Roscoe, "How to Become a Berdache" 332).

148. Jacobs 30.

149. Lang 102.

150. Califia 127.

151. Trexler 627–30. Some accounts argue that a child became a *berdache* in response to a vision and was thus exercising free will. Trexler points out that the child was prepared for the vision by adults, who explained what the child should expect and that the vision ritual was controlled, conducted and interpreted by tribal elders whose primary interest was to maintain order and authority. So it might well serve the tribe to maintain a supply of promiscuous *berdaches* to serve the needs of sexually aggressive males.

152. Lang 115.

153. See Jacobs 30, and Califia 129.

154. I set this scenario in the past because interactions today—even those on reservations—are colored by the Eurocentricity of American culture. As a further illustration of our straitjacketed understanding of sexuality, the assumption that male-on-male sexual contact constitutes homosexual behavior flies in the face of practices in other cultures. Walter Williams, who has completed extensive research or the *berdache* tradition, sites a Melanesian tribal belief that for a boy to gain manhood he must ingest semen from an older man—ideally his mother's brother. Between the ages of eight and thirteen he is placed in a house away from the village and does not interact with women. He bonds with his mentor and engages in oral and anal sex as the recipient—to reverse roles would stunt his growth. After being initiated as a man, he takes a wife and sires children. He is later expected to reverse roles and mentor a boy or boys. Williams points to this as evidence of human plasticity around sex (Williams 261–63).

155. Benedict 2.

156. Bowen 66.

157. Feinberg 35.

158. Grémaux 241.

159. Landén, et al. This information is based on responses from over 600 randomly selected Swedes. Respondents were evenly divided on the question of whether transsexuals should be allowed to raise children.

160. Cohen-Kettenis, et al. 167–9.

161. On this topic, Dr. Norman Spack observes, "I look over at the Dutch, who have 73 people whom they've treated. Not one has

changed their mind because they screen them so well. And they're the appropriate height. The females have never menstruated. They don't slice their arms because of every period they have. The genetic males do not end up with male voices. They do not end up with male height. They do not end up with an Adam's apple. … And they don't spend a half a million dollars in their lifetime on electrolysis" Adams.

162. Motmans 57. It is worth noting that Motmans published in 2010. I have not been able to ascertain whether the Netherlands has revised policies to align them with the Yogyakarta Principles as of this publication.

163. Motmans 56. The full text of the Yogyakarta Principles is available at http://www.yogyakartaprinciples.org/principles_en.htm.

164. International Commission on Civil Rights.

165. International Commission on Civil Rights 20–23. There is the possibility of extremely rare exceptions in states that rely on case law rather than legislation for civil policy. Although Austria, Germany and the Netherlands do not require divorce before gender reassignment surgery, none of these states allows a married person to officially change gender in civil records.

166. Parents of young children may find this distinction of little solace. For example, participation in scholastic and recreational athletic leagues and other activities often requires the family to file a copy of a child's birth certificate as proof of age. Although it might be possible to maintain your child's privacy through an agreement with those in charge of certifying age, there are situations in which privacy cannot be guaranteed. I remember, for example, the birth certificate requirement for Cadence's participation in a summer baseball league for ages 10-12. The league was obligated to retain a copy of each player's birth certificate and to show it to umpires and opposing coaches upon request. In our case, this presented no problem since Cadence was still Jared at the time. Of course, in accordance with the gender binary, if she had identified as female at that age, she would have been obligated to play softball and as a natal male would almost certainly have been banned from participation in that sport.

167. As mentioned in chapter two, those states are California, Colorado, Connecticut, Hawaii, Iowa, Maine, Maryland, Massachusetts, Minnesota, Missouri, New Jersey, Nevada, New

Mexico, Oregon, Vermont, Washington, and the District of Columbia.

168. O'Flaherty and Fisher 243–46.

169. An assortment of people has engaged in this debate. They include transgender activists, parents of gender-nonconforming children, endocrinologists, and surgeons, as well as therapists, and they provide a variety of nuanced arguments about the inclusion, revision, use and abuse of GID/GIDC. My intention is to provide the primary points of contention. Granted, I have chosen to explain it from a rather simplistic, two-box perspective, which is ironic, given content of chapter one, but it is beyond the scope of this discussion to provide an exhaustive explanation of the debate.

170. McHugh 38. McHugh would disagree with the point made in the next paragraph. He believes that gender reassignment surgery does nothing but harm for patients, adding to their turmoil.

171. Zucker and Bradley 266–67. Zucker has published his position clearly. He writes: "I would argue that it is as legitimate to want to make youngsters comfortable with their gender identity (to make it correspond to the physical reality of their biological sex) as it is to make youngsters comfortable with their ethnic identity (to make it correspond to the physical reality of the color of their skin). If the primary goal of treatment is to alleviate the suffering of the individual, there are now a variety of data sets that suggest that persistent gender dysphoria, at least when it continues into adolescence, is unlikely to be alleviated in the majority of cases by psychological means, and thus is likely best treated by hormonal and physical contra-sex interventions, particularly after a period of living in the cross-gender role indicates that this will result in the best adaptation for the adolescent male or female. In childhood, however, the evidence suggests that there is a much greater plasticity in outcome. As a result, many clinicians, and I am one of them, take the position that a trial of psychological treatment, including individual therapy and parent counseling, is warranted" (Zucker 550).

172. The proposed revisions can be followed at http://www.dsm5.org/ProposedRevisions/Pages/proposedrevision.aspx?rid=192#.

173. Hill, Rozanski, Carfagnini, et al. 31.

174. Gay rights activists protested at the APA's national convention in 1970 and interrupted it in 1971, calling for the removal of homosexuality from the DSM. The APA responded in 1973, replacing homosexuality with SOD, "sexual orientation disturbance." In 1980, SOD was replaced with "ego-dystonic homosexuality." The current DSM-IV-TR still includes a diagnosis that could be interpreted as pathologizing homosexuality: "sexual disorder not otherwise specified." Even the most stalwart recertifier would acknowledge that these alterations were the direct result of the uproar from gay rights advocates.
175. Zucker and Spitzer 38–9.
176. Kleinplatz and Moser 137. Spitzer was referring specifically to removal of paraphilias, not GID, but his concern about public relations belies his decades-old insistence on the separation of culture from the DSM.

WORKS CITED

Adams, Celene. "Born in a Bind: Treating Transgender Children." *Gay, Lesbian Times*, no. 1034 (October 2007). Http://www.gaylesbiantimes.com/?id=10795.

APA Task Force on Appropriate Therapeutic Responses to Sexual Orientation. *Report of the Task Force on Appropriate Therapeutic Responses to Sexual Orientation*. Washington, DC: American Psychological Association, 2009.

APA Task Force on Gender Identity and Gender Variance. *Report of the Task Force on Gender Identity and Gender Variance*. Washington, D. C.: American Psychological Association, 2008.

Bem, Sandra L. *The Lenses of Gender: Transforming the Debate on Sexual Inequality*. New Haven: Yale University Press, 1993.

Benedict, Ruth. *Patterns of Culture*. New York: Houghton Mifflin, 1934.

Bockting, Walter O., and Eli Coleman. "Developmental Stages of the Transgender Coming-Out Process: Toward an Integrated Identity." In *Principles of Transgender Medicine and Surgery*, edited by Randi Ettner, Stan Monstrey, and A. Evan Eyler, 185–208. New York: Haworth Press, 2007.

Bornstein, Kate. *Gender Outlaw: On Men, Women and the Rest of Us*. New York: Routledge, 1994.

Bowen, Gary. "An Entire Rainbow of Possibilities." In *Trans Liberation: Beyond Pink and Blue*, Leslie Feinberg, 63–66. Boston: Beacon Press, 1998.

Brill, Stephanie, and Rachel Pepper. *The Transgender Child: A Handbook for Families and Professionals*. San Francisco, CA: Cleis Press, 2008.

Bullough, Vern L., and Bonnie Bullough. *Cross-Dressing, Sex, and Gender*. Philadelphia: University of Pennsylvania Press, 1993.

Burke, Phyllis. *Gendershock: Exploding the Myths of Male and Female.* New York: Doubleday, 1996.

Califia, Patrick. *Sex Changes: The Politics of Transgenderism.* San Francisco: Cleis Press, 2003.

Chiu, Sandy W., Shannon Gervan, Courtney Fairbrother, Laurel L. Johnson, Allison F. H. Owen-Anderson, Susan J. Bradley, and Kenneth J. Zucker. "Sex-Dimorphic Color Preference in Children with Gender Identity Disorder: A Comparison to Clinical and Community Controls." *Sex Roles* 55, no. 5/6 (September 2006): 385–95.

Coates, Susan, and Ethel S. Person. "Extreme Boyhood Femininity: Isolated Behavior or Pervasive Disorder?" *Journal of the American Academy of Child Psychiatry* 24, no. 6 (November 1985): 702–9.

Cohen-Kettenis, Peggy T., and Friedemann Pfäfflin. *Transgenderism and Intersexuality in Childhood and Adolescence: Making Choices.* Developmental Clinical Psychology and Psychiatry. Thousand Oaks, CA: Sage Publications, 2003.

Costa, LeeRay M., and Andrew J. Matzner. *Male Bodies, Women's Souls: Personal Narratives of Thailand's Transgendered Youth.* New York: Haworth Press, 2007.

de Lacoste-Utamsing, Christine, and Ralph L. Holloway. "Sexual Dimorphism in the Human Corpus Callosum." *Science* 216, no. 4553 (June 1982): 1431–32.

De Sutter, Paul, K. Kira, A. Verschoor, and A. Hotimsky. "The Desire to Have Children and the Preservation of Fertility in Transsexual Women: A Survey." *International Journal of Transgenderism* 6, no. 3 (2002): 1.

Denny, Dallas. "Changing Models of Transsexualism." In *Transgender Subjectivities: A Clinician's Guide*, edited by Ubaldo Leli and Jack Drescher, 25–40. Binghamton, NY: Haworth Medical Press, 2004.

Diamond, Milton. "Biased-Interaction Theory of Psychosexual Development: 'How Does One Know If One is Male or Female?'." *Sex Roles* 55, no. 9/10 (November 2006): 589–600.

Fausto-Sterling, Anne. *Sexing the Body: Gender Politics and the Construction of Sexuality.* New York: Basic Books, 2000.

Feinberg, Leslie. *Trans Liberation: Beyond Pink or Blue.* Boston: Beacon Press, 1998.

———. *Transgender Warriors: Making History from Joan of Arc to RuPaul.* Boston: Beacon Press, 1996.

Fisher, Roger, and William Ury. *Getting to Yes: Negotiating Agreement Without Giving In.* New York, N.Y.: Penguin Books, 1983.

Gibb, Jack R. "Defensive Communication." *Journal of Communication* 11 (1961): 141–48.

Goffman, Erving. "The Arrangement Between the Sexes." *Theory & Society* 4, no. 3 (Fall 1977): 301–31.

Green, Richard. *Sexual Identity Conflict in Children and Adults.* New York: Basic Books, 1974.

———. *The "Sissy Boy Syndrome" and the Development of Homosexuality.* New Haven: Yale University Press, 1987.

Grémaux, René. "Woman Becomes Man in the Balkans." In *Third Sex, Third Gender: Beyond Sexual Dimorphism in Culture and History*, Gilbert Herdt, 241–81. New York: Zone Books, 1994.

Hall, Kira. "'Go Suck Your Husband's Sugarcane!': Hijras and the Use of Sexual Insult." In *Queerly Phrased: Language, Gender, and Sexuality*, edited by Anna Livia and Kira Hall, 430–60. New York: Oxford University Press, 1997.

Hill, Darryl B., Christina Rozanski, Jessica Carfagnini, and Brian Willoughby. "Gender Identity Disorders in Childhood and Adolescence: A Critical Inquiry." *Journal of Psychology and Human Sexuality* 7, no. 3–4 (2005): 7–33, edited by Dan Karasic and Jack Drescher. Binghamton, NY: Haworth Press.

Horton, Mary Ann. "Incidence and Prevalence of SRS Among US Residents." Unpublished paper, 2008. Http://www.tgender.net/taw/thb/THBPrevalence-OE2008.pdf.

Hubbard, Ruth. *The Politics of Women's Biology.* New Brunswick, NJ: Rutgers University Press, 1990.

Hyman, Iris. *Self-Disclosure and Its Impact on Individuals Who Receive Mental Health Services.* HHS Pub. No. (SMA)-08–4337. Rockville, MD: U.S. Department of Health and Human Services. Center for Mental Health Services, Substance Abuse and Mental Health Services Administation, 2008. Http://download.ncadi.samhsa.gov/ken/pdf/SMA08–4337/SelfDisclosure_50p.pdf.

International Commission on Civil Rights. *Transsexualism in Europe.* Strasbourg, Germany: Council of Europe, 2000.

Israel, Gianna E., and Donald E. Tarver. *Transgender Care: Recommended Guidelines, Practical Information, and Personal Accounts.* Philadelphia: Temple University Press, 1997.

Jacobs, Sue-Ellen. "Is the 'North American Berdache' Merely a Phantom of the Imagination of Western Social Scientists?" In *Two-Spirit People: Native American Gender Identity, Sexuality, and Spirituality*, edited by Sue-Ellen Jacobs, Wesley Thomas, and Sabine Lang, 21–43. Urbana: University of Illinois Press, 1997.

Kelly, Anita E. "Revealing Personal Secrets." *Current Directions in Psychological Science* 8, no. 9 (August p. 105–108. 1999): 105–8.

Kelly, Anita E., Julie A. Klusas, Renee T. von Weiss, and Christine Kenny. "What is It About Revealing Secrets That is Beneficial?" *Personality and Social Psychology Bulletin* 27, no. 6 (June 2001): 651–65.

Kleinplatz, Peggy J., and Charles Moser. "Politics Versus Science: An Addendum and Response to Drs. Spitzer and Fink." *Journal of Psychology & Human Sexuality* 17, no. 3/4 (2005): 135–39.

Kruijver Frank.P., Jiang-Ning Zhou, Chris. W. Pool., Michael A. Hofman, Louis J. Gooren, and Dick F. Swaab. "Male-to-Female Transsexuals Have Female Neuron Numbers in a Limbic Nucleus." *The Journal Of Clinical Endocrinology And Metabolism* 85, no. 5 (May 2000): 2034–41.

Kubany, Edward S., David C. Richard, Gordon B. Bauer, and Miles Y. Muraoka. "Impact of Assertive and Accusatory Communication of Distress and Anger: A Verbal Component Analysis." *Aggressive Behavior* 18, no. 5 (1992): 337–47.

Ladd-Taylor, Molly, and Lauri Umansky, eds. *"Bad" Mothers: The Politics of Blame in Twentieth-Century America.* New York: New York University Press, 1998.

Landén, Mikael, and Sune Innala. "Attitudes toward Transsexualism in a Swedish National Survey." *Archives of Sexual Behavior* 29, no. 4 (August 2000): 375–88.

Lang, Sabine. "Various Kinds of Two-Spirit People: Gender Variance and Homosexuality in Native American Communities." In *Two-Spirit People: Native American Gender Identity, Sexuality, and Spirituality*, edited by Sue-Ellen Jacobs, Wesley Thomas, and Sabine Lang, 100–118. Urbana: University of Illinois Press, 1997.

Lev, Arlene Istar. *Transgender Emergence: Therapeutic Guidelines for Working with Gender-Variant People and Their Families*. New York: The Haworth Clinical Practice Press, 2004.

———— and Laura Alie. "Trangender and Gender Noncornforming Children and Youth: Developing a Culturally Competent System of Care." In *Improving Emotional and Behavioral Outcomes for LGBT Youth: A Guide for Professionals*, edited by Sylvia K. Fisher, Jeffrey M. Poirer, and Gary M. Blau, 43-66. Baltimore: Paul H. Brookes, 2012.

Lippa, Richard A. *Gender, Nature, and Nurture*. Mahwah, N.J.: Lawrence Erlbaum Associates, 2005.

Lothstein, Leslie M. *Female-to-Male Transsexualism: Historical, Clinical, and Theoretical Issues*. Boston: Routledge & Kegan Paul, 1983.

————. "Psychodynamics and Sociodynamics of Gender-Dysphoric States." *American Journal Of Psychotherapy* 33, no. 2 (April 1979): 214–38.

MacKenzie, Gordene Olga. *Transgender Nation*. Bowling Green, OH: Bowling Green State University Popular Press, 1994.

McHugh, Paul. "Surgical Sex." *First Things: A Monthly Journal of Religion & Public Life*, no. 147 (November 2004): 34–38. The Institute on Religion and Public Life.

McLafferty, Jr., Charles L. "Examining Unproven Assumptions of Galton's Nature-Nurture Paradigm." *American Psychologist* 61, no. 2 (February/March 2006): 177–78.

Mead, Margaret. *Sex and Temperament in Three Primitive Societies*. New York: W. Morrow & company, 1935.

Menvielle, Edgardo J. "Gender Identity Disorder: Comment on S. J. Bradley and K. J. Zucker." Letter to the editor. *Journal of the American Academy of Child and Adolescent Psychiatry* 37, no. 3 (March 1998): 243–44.

Meyerowitz, Joanne J. *How Sex Changed: A History of Transsexuality in the United States*. Cambridge, MA: Harvard University Press, 2002.

Motmans, Joz. *Being Transgender* Jiang-Ning *in Belgium: Mapping the Social and Legal Situation of Transgender People*. Brussels: Institute for the Equality of Women and Men, 2010. Http://igvm-iefh.belgium.be/nl/binaries/34%20-%20Transgender_ENG_tcm336–99783.pdf.

Nanda, Serena. "Hijras: An Alternative Sex and Gender Role in India." In *Third Sex, Third Gender: Beyond Sexual Dimorphism in Culture and History*, edited by Gilbert Herdt, 374–417. New York: Zone Books, 1994.

Nemoto, Tooru, Don Operario, JoAnne Keatley, Lei Han, and Toho Soma. "HIV Risk Behaviors among Male-to-Female Transgender Persons of Color in San Francisco." *American Journal of Public Health* 94, no. 7 (July 2004): 1193–1119.

O'Flaherty, Michael, and John Fisher. "Sexual Orientation, Gender Identity and International Human Rights Law: Contextuatlizing the Yogyakarta Principles." *Human Rights Law Review* 8, no. 2 (2008): 207–48.

Pennebaker, James W. *Opening up: The Healing Power of Expressing Emotions*. New York: William Morrow, 1990.

Ravaging the Vulnerable: Abuses against Persons of High Risk of HIV Infection in Bangladesh. Human Rights Watch, 2003.

Rekers, George A. "Assessment and Treatment Methods for Gender Identity Disorders and Transvestism." In *Handbook of Child and Adolescent Sexual Problems*. Series in Scientific Foundations of Clinical and Counseling Psychology, 272–89. New York: Lexington Books, 1995.

Rekers, George A., and Mark D. Kilgus. "Differential Diagnosis and Rationale of Treatment of Gender Identity Disorders and Transvestism." In *Handbook of Child and Adolescent Sexual Problems*. Series in Scientific Foundations of Clinical and Counseling Psychology, 255–71. New York: Lexington Books, 1995.

Ridley, Matt. *Nature Via Nurture: Genes, Experience, and What Makes Us Human*. New York, N.Y.: HarperCollins, 2003.

Rodriguez, Robert R., and Anita E. Kelly. "Health Effects of Disclosing Secrets to Imagined Accepting Versus Nonaccepting Confidants." *Journal of Social and Clinical Psychology* 25, no. 9 (2006): 1023–47.

Roscoe, Will. *Changing Ones: Third and Fourth Genders in Native North America*. New York: St. Martin's Press, 1998.

———. "How to Become a Berdache: Toward a Unified Analysis of Gender Diversity." In *Third Sex, Third Gender: Beyond Sexual Dimorphism in Culture and History*, edited by Gilbert Herdt, 329–72. New York: Zone Books, 1994.

Rubin, Henry. *Self-Made Men: Identity and Embodiment among Transsexual Men.* Nashville: Vanderbilt University Press., 2003.

Rutter, Michael. *Genes and Behavior: Nature — Nurture Interplay Explained.* Malden, MA: Blackwell, 2006.

Schaefer, Leah Cahan, and Connie Christine Wheeler. "Guilt in Cross-Gender Identity Conditions: Presentations and Treatment." In *Transgender Subjectivites; a Clinician's Guide*, edited by Ubaldo Leli and Jack Drescher, 117–27. Binghamton, NY: Haworth Medical Press, 2004.

Spiegel, Alix, ed. and comp. Review of in *Parents Consider Treatment to Delay Son's Puberty: New Therapy Would Buy Time to Resolve Gender Crisis.* Radio program segment. All Things Considered. National Public Radio, 2008. Http://www.npr.org/templates/story/story.php?storyId=90234780.

Stoller, Robert J. *Presentations of Gender.* New Haven: Yale University Press, 1985.

Stotz, Karola. "The Ingredients for a Postgenomic Synthesis of Nature and Nurture." *Philosophical Psychology* 21, no. 3 (June 2008): 359–81.

Stuart, Kim Elizabeth. *The Uninvited Dilemma: A Question of Gender.* Portland, OR: Metamorphous Press, 1991.

Swaab, Dick. F. "Sexual Differentiation of the Human Brain: Relevance for Gender Identity, Transsexualism and Sexual Orientation." *Gynecological Endocrinology* 19, no. 6 (December 2004): 301–12.

Terry, Jennifer. "'Momism' and the Making of Treasonous Homosexuals." In *"Bad" Mothers: The Politics of Blame in Twentieth-Century America*, edited by Molly Ladd-Taylor and Lauri Umansky, 169–90. New York: New York University Press, 1998.

Thomas, Kenneth. "Conflict and Conflict Management." In *Handbook of Industrial and Organizational Psychology*, edited by Marvin Dunnette, 890–934. Chicago: Rand McNally, 1976.

Thorne, Barrie. *Gender Play: Girls and Boys in School.* New Brunswick, NJ: Rutgers University Press, 1993.

Trexler, Richard C. "Making of the American Berdache: Choice or Constraint?" *Journal of Social History* 35, no. 3 (Spring 2002): 613–36.

Veale, Jaimie F., David E. Clarke, Terri C. Lomax, and 2. "Biological and Psychosocial Correlates of Adult Gender-Variant Identities: A Review." *Personality & Individual Differences* 48, no. 4 (March 2010): 357–66.

Verderber, Kathleen, and Rudolph Verderber. *Inter-Act: Interpersonal Communication, Concepts, Skills, and Contexts.* Belmont, CA: Wadsworth, 2001.

Wallien, Madeleine S. C., and Peggy T. Cohen-Kettenis. "Psychosexual Outcome of Gender-Dysphoric Children." *Journal of the American Academy of Child & Adolescent Psychiatry* 47, no. 12 (December 2008): 1413–23.

West, Merideth J., and Andrew P. King. "Settling Nature and Nurture into an Ontogenetic Niche." *Developmental Psychobiology* 20, no. 5 (September 1987): 549–62.

Williams, Kipling D., and Lara Dolnik. "Revealing the Worst First: Stealing Thunder as a Social Influence Strategy." In *Social Influence: Direct and Indirect Processes*, edited by Joseph P. Forgas and Kipling D. Williams, 213–31. Philadelphia: Psychology Press, 2001.

Williams, Walter L. *The Spirit and the Flesh: Sexual Diversity in American Indian Culture.* Boston: Beacon Press, 1986.

Willis, Irene. "Pronouns." In *At the Fortune Cafe*, 44. Valdosto, GE: Snake Nation Press, 2005.

Winter, Sam. "Transphobia, a Price Worth Paying for Gender Identity Disorder?" Conference presentation. First World Congress for Sexual Health (18th Congress of the World Association for Sexology). Sydney, Australia, 2007. Http://web.hku.hk/~sjwinter/TransgenderASIA/WAS2007paper.htm.

Winter, Sam, and Nuttawuk Udomsak. "Male, Female and Transgender : Stereotypes and Self in Thailand." *The International Journal of Transgenderism* 6, no. 1 (January-March 2002). Http://www.symposion.com/ijt/ijtvo06no01_04.htm.

World Professional Association for Transgender Health (WPATH). "Standards of Care for the Health of Transsexual, Transgender, and Gender Nonconforming People," 2011.

Wylie, Philip. *Generation of Vipers..* New York: Rinehart, 1942.

Xavier Jessica M., Marilyn Bobbin, Ben Singer , and Earline Budd. "A Needs Assessment of Transgendered People of Color Living in

Washington, DC." *International Journal of Transgenderism* 8, no. 2/3 (2005): 31–47.

Zucker, Kenneth J. "Commentary on Langer and Martin's (2004) "How Dresses Can Make You Mentally Ill: Examining Gender Identity Disorder in Children"." *Child and Adolescent Social Work Journal* 23, no. 5–6 (December 2006): 533–55.

———. "Gender Identity Disorders in Children: Clinical Descriptions and Natural History." In *Clinical Management of Gender Identity Disorders in Children and Adults*, edited by Ray Blanchard and Betty W. Steiner, 3–23. Washington, D.C.: American Psychiatric Press, 1990.

———. "On the 'Natural History' of Gender Identity Disorder in Children." *Journal of the American Academy of Child and Adolescent Psychiatry* 27, no. 12 (December 2008): 1312–63.

Zucker, Kenneth J., and Susan J. Bradley. *Gender Identity Disorder and Psychosexual Problems in Children and Adolescents*. New York: Guilford Press, 1995.

Zucker, Kenneth J., and Robert L. Spitzer. "Was the Gender Identity Disorder of Childhood Diagnosis Introduced Into DSM-III as a Backdoor Maneuver to Replace Homosexuality? A Historical Note." *Journal of Sex & Marital Therapy* 31 (2005): 31–42.1.

INDEX

CPSIA information can be obtained at www.ICGtesting.com
Printed in the USA
BVOW030351170513

320951BV00006B/13/P